# Kindercoding Unplugged

# Kindercoding Unplugged

## SCREEN-FREE
### Activities for Beginners

Deanna Pecaski McLennan, PhD

**Redleaf Press®**
www.redleafpress.org
800-423-8309

Published by Redleaf Press
10 Yorkton Court
St. Paul, MN 55117
www.redleafpress.org

First edition 2020
Senior editor: Melissa York
Managing editor: Douglas Schmitz
Cover design: Danielle Carnito
Cover photograph: Deanna Pecaski McLennan
Interior design: Percolator Graphic Design
Typeset in Novel Pro
Printed in the United States of America
27  26  25  24  23  22  21  20      1  2  3  4  5  6  7  8

Library of Congress Cataloging-in-Publication Data

Names: McLennan, Deanna Pecaski, author.
Title: Kindercoding unplugged : screen-free activities for beginners / Deanna Pecaski McLennan.
Description: First edition. | St. Paul, MN : Redleaf Press, 2020. | Includes bibliographical refer-
    ences and index. | Summary: "Many programs and schools understand the importance of
    teaching twenty-first-century competencies, but when it comes to coding, many educators
    feel lost. This book aims to bridge that knowledge gap by providing the support and encour-
    agement in order to get started with coding in classrooms"—Provided by publisher.
Identifiers: LCCN 2020007470 (print) | LCCN 2020007471 (ebook) | ISBN 9781605547091
    (paperback) | ISBN 9781605547107 (ebook)
Subjects: LCSH: Computer programming—Study and teaching (Early childhood) |
    Early childhood education—Activity programs. | Reggio Emilia approach (Early childhood
    education) | Computers and children.
Classification: LCC LB1139.35.C64 M35 2020 (print) | LCC LB1139.35.C64 (ebook) |
    DDC 004.083—dc23
LC record available at https://lccn.loc.gov/2020007470
LC ebook record available at https://lccn.loc.gov/2020007471


Printed on acid-free paper

For Cadence, Caleb, and Quinn

who bring happiness and love to my life each day
and help me see the world with childhood joy and wonder

Coding is today's language of creativity.
All our children deserve a chance to become creators
instead of consumers of computer science.

—Maria Klawe

# Contents

# CHAPTER 1

# From Following a Map to Coding Our Own Journey

*The children were obsessed with maps—treasure maps, road maps, globes, floor plans of the school, maps of the neighborhood and even the country. Everywhere you looked there were maps. Children were drawing them at the writing center, reading about them in library books, bringing them from home, exploring Google Earth, and incorporating them into their dramatic play outside. And although one would think that this would be the start of an exploration of community or country, it ultimately led our class on a yearlong inquiry into coding.*

## From Maps to Coding

I am a Reggio Emilia–inspired kindergarten educator in Southern Ontario, Canada. Over the course of a week, I had noticed that the children were fixated on maps. It had started one day when a student named Sawyer brought a map to school after visiting Canada's Wonderland (a theme park filled with roller coasters and more) the weekend before. I think the novelty of the map was in its unknown—in a time of GPS and smart devices, I doubt that very many children had witnessed their parents using paper maps to navigate travel in the car. I recall the excitement a map could inspire in my childhood: nights before long trips filled with discussions about the places we'd see as I would listen to my parents planning and watch my father smooth out the wrinkles of our well-loved provincial map and trace our journey with his finger. That map seemed so big, so impossible to me back then. Were we really going to travel that far in just a week?

I believed the children's same thrill existed in their play with the maps. The idea of imagining what fantastical destinations awaited them after their long journeys was riveting, helping children to suspend disbelief and embrace their roles within the context of the play. Stories of adventure, heroism, and discovery punctuated their activities. Each time they'd race by me on their tricycles, maps in hand, shouting directions to the next castle or port of call, I'd have to stop what I was doing and watch. The map, you see, is not a location tool or play prop. It is a language of understanding and communication, a symbolic code no different than the writing on these pages or numbers used in equations.

A child-drawn map displaying locations relevant to his imaginary, dramatic play.

## Emergent Learning

As an educator, I use children's interests to guide our classroom programming. Over the course of that week, I had observed and documented the children's mapping activities in a variety of ways to uncover the depths of their learning. I was curious about their explorations and wanted to learn more. Educators who embrace child-initiated inquiries in the classroom are researchers—asking questions, gathering data, and planning how to proceed in the quest for deeper understanding. I photocopied their drawings, studied their writing, asked them questions about their play, transcribed their conversations, took photos and videos of their role playing, and planned how to heighten their explorations and embed rich learning opportunities within their playful explorations. Not wanting to default to the safe and familiar (a logical inquiry might include studying community and location after noticing the maps in the play), I looked for outside inspiration. I was familiar with the coding the older children in our school were doing and was curious to learn what it was all about. I had been waiting for an opportunity to meaningfully integrate it within the children's play, and I knew the interest in maps was the spark I needed.

There was just one slight issue—I had no experience with coding. At the time, I was embracing authentic math experiences and looking for activities to engage children in rich thinking that grew their confidence and mindset and helped them see the relevance of math to their immediate world. As part of my own personal professional development, I was devouring everything I could read regarding building math capacity in early childhood. One text, *Taking Shape* (Moss et al. 2016), stood out to me because of its emphasis on the importance of spatial reasoning. In this text, an introduction to unplugged coding is provided with sample activities to try in the classroom. I knew that math confidence and achievement were directly related to positive growth mindset and wanted to embed activities in our classroom that promoted collaborative problem-solving and risk-taking in a safe and supportive space (Boaler 2016). Intrigued, I had wanted to try something similar and felt it was an ideal time. Not letting my lack of coding experience or confidence get in our way, I jumped in fully, knowing that learning can sometimes be messy and spontaneous for both children *and* educators. I felt I didn't have to be a master programmer before using coding in the classroom. I would just learn right along with the children. Taking risks in the past has often led us on some of our most meaningful and exciting projects, so I knew to place trust in the process and see what happened. For example, one year the children were interested in observing the life cycle of a praying mantis up close. Despite my reluctance to keep the creature in a terrarium in our classroom, the excitement of watching dozens of babies hatch from the egg sack and the rich math that it inspired in children was worth the price of my inexperience and discomfort.

I also knew that it was important to engage children in coding activities because I was unsure of the exposure they had to high-quality technology in their homes. Some children had regular access and were quite knowledgeable and proficient. However, I also knew that regular access does not always equate to rich learning, as many children spend hours with a device each day, playing rote games or watching entertainment videos. Engaging children in complex computational thinking using coding would ensure that technology, even though unplugged, could equalize the playing field and encourage children to become critical thinkers and technological producers instead of passive users.

The next day, we spent time during whole-group circle reflecting on our map play. I displayed photos and videos of the children's explorations from the previous days and asked them to think about and share what was happening in each piece of documentation. After our conversation, I introduced an unplugged coding board to the children by placing it in the middle of our carpet. I had created a simple grid using a piece of plexiglass and sectioned it off with masking tape. As I presented the board to the children, I asked them to describe what they saw and to suggest what it might be useful for. The children's answers were varied—they hypothesized it was a new game to play, it was something that could be used outside, it looked like a maze—and then someone suggested that it reminded them of a map. Many children nodded in agreement, and the children described how the grid could be transformed to represent location. Everyday play objects, including blocks and magnetic tiles, could be used on top to depict structures and landmarks (making it topographical), real photos could be placed underneath (creating maps similar to what we had observed on Google Earth), or drawings could be inserted into the different squares to show certain areas (like the coordinate games we had played before). Following their lead, we gathered materials and set to work. I wasn't sure of where our activities would take us, but the power of inquiry lies in trusting in the children and the process and providing support and encouragement along the way. The children buzzed with excitement and were eager to incorporate the grid into that day's explorations. And as the room hummed with the sound of their planning, I knew that something big had taken hold. I recognized the sound and feel of a rich inquiry taking root and couldn't wait to see where this new adventure would lead us, with the coding grid now becoming our new map into the unknown. My intuition that day was right. Computational thinking overtook our classroom, and over the course of that year, we spent much time incorporating unplugged coding into our explorations.

## Unplugged Coding

Computer programming is a basic language of the digital age. Computer programmers use machine code, which is specific sequences of binary numbers, to give directions to computers. A computer uses these step-by-step instructions to run programs. Gaming systems, tablets, cars, cell phones, and even washing machines all use code to function properly. However, I was not interested in providing opportunities for the children to code using a device. I wanted them to explore the concept of coding, and acquire all the benefits that computational thinking offered, without screen time. Unplugged coding is when children use familiar tools, not wired technology, to practice coding. It does not use computers or screen time. Unplugged coding engages children in activities that incorporate computational thinking—creativity, collaboration, pattern recognition, perseverance, and creation. It emphasizes metacognition, problem-solving, and abstract thinking through interactive and approachable games and activities that are physically, not digitally, manipulated by players. Not all children will grow to be computer programmers, yet all children should have the opportunity to engage in opportunities that help them explore computational thinking. Not only does it help prepare children for the world we live in today (after all, chances are that some children will grow up to have a job in the tech field), unplugged coding teaches many other valuable skills, as well as helping fulfill many of the standards for math practice as outlined in the Common Core. Coding is a vehicle that helps bring children's ideas to life and transfers these beyond the student, enabling them to be read and used by others around the world. These twenty-first-century competencies can be grouped into three main categories, as described by the National Research Council (2012):

> **Cognitive** competencies include critical thinking, decision making, creativity, innovation, problem-solving, active listening, and adaptive learning.

> **Interpersonal** competencies include negotiation, teamwork, empathy, collaboration, conflict resolution, self-presentation, and cooperation.

> **Intrapersonal** competencies include adaptability, integrity, productivity, initiative, continuous learning, grit, perseverance, and artistic and cultural appreciation.

Just as our maps inspired rich, imaginative role play and journeys across land and sea, the children's coding was a complex and long-term project in our classroom. Regardless of what shape future projects took, coding emerged time and time again. I noticed that with each experience, children seemed to acquire complex math and literacy skills while becoming more confident and committed to their work. Student intention behind the coding became more evident with each subsequent practice, and over time the children, not adults, were directing their work. I was able to integrate more sophisticated coding concepts as the children became more proficient. Coding also transformed my role as an educator; I was able to see deep connections between computational thinking, my Reggio Emilia–inspired practice, and the use of authentic math and literacy tasks in our classroom. As the year progressed, I tweeted our activities regularly (@McLennan1977) and shared many of our classroom explorations through professional writing and presentations to put children's faces on the coding experience and help bring their ideas to the rest of the world (Pecaski McLennan 2017a; 2017b). Our coding work caught on quickly. Many educators were curious to know how unplugged coding worked and how they could also integrate a coding framework into their classroom lessons and activities as well. Some educators assumed that confidence using computers was a necessary requirement and shied away, while others worried their limited technical skills would not be able to keep up.

The more I spoke to educators, the faster a sense of urgency grew inside of me to share our success and encourage all educators to find a place for computational-thinking activities in their classrooms. If we introduce unplugged coding games in the early primary years, children will become more confident and proficient using computational skills and strategies. Just as emergent spaces encourage children to personalize their learning through multifaceted sensory experiences, technology gives children one more of the "hundreds of languages" through which to explore, experiment, and communicate their ideas to others. I want all children to be able to think and speak in algorithms (Wein 2014).

Many educators confuse coding with passive entertainment-style gaming and worry that it will be a harmful distraction in the early primary classroom. What I found is that unplugged coding, and other computational activities, are highly suitable to inquiry-based programs and can be used in many different ways. Coding can become one of the children's languages, used as a means of exploration and communication in a variety of learning domains. It can be a teacher-provided invitation, introduced during whole group time and left to be explored during center time. It can also be a spontaneous response to an interest expressed freely by a child during play. Coding is extremely adaptable, and children's interest and abilities grow with practice.

Coding is also highly conducive to a variety of learning domains and modalities. Many people confuse the experience of coding with the critical thinking and problem-solving skills it encourages in learners. It's not the act of coding but the thinking within the coding that is important: the multifaceted learning environment that coding promotes is what we are striving to create in the classroom for all children. Not a place of predictability and rote routines, but an exciting space where children can't wait to step through the door and see what engaging learning possibilities are available that day. Coding is simply the mode one uses to engage children in complex computational-thinking experiences that can adapt and evolve over time (Umaschi Bers 2018).

Being able to articulate the pedagogy behind our practice is important—why we are choosing coding as an activity for math and literacy instead of more traditional lessons—especially when faced with questions from resistant or reluctant administrators, colleagues, and families. Coding is a newer idea to education, one that many adults may not have had previous experiences with or understandings of. Deconstructing computational activities and making the learning visible every step of the way is important for building support and trust for its implementation into your program. Just as coders use **modularity** to break down activities or procedures into simpler, more manageable parts that create a powerful idea or process when combined, educators must be able to dissect the process of coding to adequately explain and justify its potential for powerful learning and see how these small pieces all fit together. Being able to articulate the standards you are fulfilling through a solid educational framework gives you credibility and helps bring along more hesitant educators who might be willing to give it a try.

## Coding for the Twenty-First-Century Classroom

Regular coding experiences can transform educators, helping them recognize the potential for complex learning by embracing the unknown and valuing the process, not just the product, of student explorations. It can strengthen teaching instruction as connections are formed between unplugged coding and rich, authentic math and literacy experiences. It may give educators the confidence to take risks in their teaching and try something new. Unplugged coding creates a space for educators to become colearners with the children, modeling patience and perseverance in our collaborative problem-solving. I believe that every child should be provided the time, environment, and resources to engage in meaningful computational thinking in the classroom. Coding should be a right for every educator and child. After my time exploring coding with children, I arrived at a number of reasons why it needs to be an essential component of the twenty-first-century classroom:

> **Coding is everywhere.** Most appliances and everyday household items require code to work. When children learn about coding, they acquire a sense of how the world around them functions.

> **Coding is easy once you understand the basics.** An educator does not need to know computer programming to use coding activities. Starting slowly and exploring together with the children will model curiosity and a willingness to take risks while helping teacher-learners build community and knowledge in a safe and supportive space.

> **Coding is cost-effective.** In a time of reduced budgets and tech constraints, unplugged coding requires no computers to be successful. All one really needs to start is a grid, arrow coding cards, and small props (such as blocks or animal figures). These materials can be easily made or found around the classroom and are transportable to other areas of the school (like the hallway or outdoors).

> **Coding activities naturally incorporate twenty-first-century skills.** Children who code experience collaboration, creativity, teamwork, critical thinking, and problem-solving in their activities. They quickly realize that their directions need to be clear and precise so they will have fun and be successful in the coding play. Children learn to strategize as coding play becomes more complex and obstacles and challenges are added to their

games. Algorithms that don't work out build resilience and persistence as children try new sequences and use mistakes as learning opportunities.

> **Coding integrates learning opportunities from multiple domains of development.** In our world of dense curriculum and overwhelming assessment demands, it's essential that educators weave together expectations from different subjects and strands. Coding has the potential to use expectations from math, science, literacy, the arts, and physical education, depending on the context and limits of your children's imaginations.

> **Coding is a social activity that builds communication and relationships.** Each person in the activity has a special role to play, and these roles must work together to be successful. The directions given by the programmer must be clear and succinct and followed precisely by all players involved. Children work together to create more complex coding paths. Play from one day can be continued into the next. Coding strengthens children's oral language as they describe movement while giving and receiving directions.

> **Coding provides opportunities for children to engage in meaningful, problem-based math that is highly engaging and relevant to their lives.** These activities integrate spatial awareness, patterning, reasoning, and number sense into a highly motivating opportunity for applying math in a realistic situation that can then be transferred to a coding application when children are ready (such as the Scratch Jr. app or an online Scratch game). The math is often complex and layered and helps educators fulfill expectations from multiple areas in the Common Core.

> **Coding is empowering.** Children build confidence in themselves as they experience complex coding activities in the classroom. Often these can be challenging as children problem solve through difficult situations and use their mistakes as learning opportunities. Grit and perseverance are developed as children remain with a task until completion.

> **Coding is versatile and can be easily adapted to activities in the gym and outdoor learning spaces, captivating kinesthetic learners and adding another dimension to physical activities.** It is an easy-to-adapt activity that is fun to play outside or on a very large grid. Children can code one another to move around a space or use the change in scenery to inspire a new programming narrative. Bringing these activities outside enhances the experience, as children are free to use big-body movements, loud voices, and their surroundings in the context of their work.

> **Coding can be extended with technology such as easy-to-use apps, websites, and robots for those who want to delve more deeply into the**

**concepts or offer home extensions.** Although in this text we focus primarily on screen-free coding, there are many digital extensions suitable for young children as tangible next steps for those who are ready. Many of these are available as free apps or websites and can be suggested to families who want activities that promote home-school connections, or used in subsequent activities or grades for children who are ready for the challenge.

> **Coding is a global phenomenon and connects your students to their community and beyond!** Educators can create their own personal learning networks by connecting with others worldwide on social media using coding hashtags (#coding, #21stedchat, #kindercoding, #MTBoS, #mathchat, #iteachmath). Classes can participate in the Hour of Code together with children from around the world. Children can reach out to others and share their coding games and learning with others using social media, or research new activities to play.

## The Power of Coding

Coding has taken me on an incredible journey of self-expression and risk-taking, as both an educator and a learner. I've written this book to take you along with me. In the same way the children used their maps as a guide for rich, inventive play, you can use the ideas in this book to reflect on your own pedagogy and practice and to help you see the role computational thinking can have in your emergent classroom.

I'm hoping that by sharing vignettes from my teaching practice, linking activities to an educational foundation, and showing the progression of children's thinking over time, I can convince you that coding is a way of being in the classroom. A computational atmosphere needs to be built and nurtured. It's not a series of activities you implement; it's a state of thinking and being that transforms every invested person. Traveling the path together, building your computational schema, using proper terminology in context, and weaving activities together will empower you as a learner. My hope is that this book takes you on a journey to becoming a confident producer, not just consumer, of information and technology in your life. I have also written this book for children everywhere who have a right to learn to code in their early childhood school years, just as they have a right to learn to read, write, and engage in rich mathematical experiences. I'm hoping that by sharing our journey with you, I can inspire you to live each day looking for opportunities to enrich your classroom with joyful algorithms and embrace rich moments of unplugged play and learning, regardless of what shape they might take.

**CHAPTER 2**

# Connecting Reggio Emilia to Computational Thinking

*A flurry of activity ensued as the children crowded close to the floor. A basket of Cuisenaire rods was nearby, and the children were lining them up end to end. What had started as a simple measuring activity evolved into the children working to measure the entire perimeter of the classroom. For over an hour, they meticulously lined the rods, counting as they went. When they encountered problems, such as how to navigate sharp corners, they engaged in rich conversation, referring to previous experiences and deciding as a team how to move forward. Upon first glance it might not seem like it, but this measurement task is rich with computational thinking. Working as an efficient team, the children collaborated to solve an interesting and complex problem. They were creative in their approach, incorporated previous knowledge and experience, looked for patterns in their work, and communicated clearly with others. Their initial interest in measuring was sustained over several days, and each time their approach became more confident and sophisticated as they learned from their mistakes and persevered in the task.*

## What Is Computational Thinking?

For the purposes of the work presented in this book, computational thinking is defined as "the process of taking a complex problem, understanding what the problem is, and developing possible solutions. These can be explored and represented in ways that a computer, or human, or both can understand" (Bitesize 2018). There is still much debate in the computer sciences regarding the exact definition of computational thinking. Jeannette Wing (2006), a computer scientist and professor, is an advocate for the inclusion of computational thinking in the classroom as an essential component of education for every child. Reminiscent of the Reggio Emilia belief that children should be viewed as capable and driven constructors of their own realities with the right to learn and exist as a member of a democratic space, Wing believes that experiences with computational thinking are a necessity for every child. She argues, however, that computational thinking is a system by which humans, not necessarily computers, process information about the world around them and should be applied to many other disciplines. Coding exists as simply one of the languages in which communication using computational thinking can occur (Aspinall 2017; Umaschi Bers 2018). Many parallels exist between Wing's view of the learner as a coder and the process through which coders can experiment with the world around them, and the foundations of Reggio Emilia. Computational thinking has many similarities to the inquiry-based process used in emergent classrooms:

> representing problems in new and innovative ways

> organizing and analyzing different forms of information

> analyzing a problem and decomposing it into several smaller parts

> organizing a problem into a series of ordered steps

> observing, identifying, analyzing, and implementing different solutions to the problem

> identifying the most effective and efficient solution

> incorporating the problem-solving model across disciplines

As an educator, I have never been reluctant to take risks and see where the less-traveled path might take us. Passionate about improving my practice, I consider myself a learner, continually reading, writing, and researching about how to evolve myself, and our program, for the betterment of all children. Inspired by Reggio Emilia, the children in my care give shape and direction to our learning, and I follow their lead. I have always valued process-based exploration. From my roots in sociodrama (using the power of the arts for social change) to my current fascination with building student confidence and mathematical mindset, I believe in the power of embracing mistakes as opportunities for growth, and I view my classroom as a laboratory for educational research and change (Pecaski McLennan 2008, 2012). Before delving more deeply into understanding the role coding and computational thinking have had in our emergent learning, exploring some of the pedagogy behind my practice is important so that you can understand our learning environment and be encouraged to consider what educational theories have inspired your own.

## Reggio Emilia

In my teaching practice, I celebrate each child as an individual, born with an intrinsic desire to interact with and deeply understand the complexities of the immediate world and beyond. Reggio Emilia believes that children learn best through meaningful social interactions, and that they explore and communicate through

A child measures the perimeter of the classroom using Cuisenaire rods.

hundreds of symbolic languages. I use play and inquiry as the heart of our work together, and I attempt to weave children's interests, strengths, and next steps for improvement into our classroom environment and activities. As educators support and guide, they become colearners together with children, engaging in rich explorations through inquiry-based projects. Studying Reggio Emilia in depth has helped me recognize coding as one of these languages and see the deep significance and connection it can have to children's learning. When children have ideas, they desire them to be shared with a greater community, and they are able to communicate these intentions using the global language of coding. It transcends language, culture, and even time and space, and can take children's messages around the world, leading to infinite learning possibilities and positively affecting so many more children than just the original coder. Unplugged coding activities align directly with the beliefs of Reggio Emilia in many ways. Below are several examples:

> **The image of the child:** Reggio Emilia values all children as strong, competent, resilient individuals who are able to guide their own learning and build theories of understanding about how the world around them works. The classroom is considered a democratic space, and children are encouraged to build individual and collective knowledge and understanding together. Children are provided the time and space necessary to move through activities or experiences at their own pace of learning, and all

adults (educators, families, educational stakeholders) have a responsibility to support them the best they can (Wein 2014; Wurm 2005).

> **The role of the environment:** In Reggio Emilia, emphasis is placed on cultivating a safe, supportive, and aesthetic learning environment for all children. Tools and materials in the environment change and evolve based on the children's expressed interests, strengths, and needs, and they are intentionally selected to support deeper exploration in student-driven projects. Coding is not just a cognitive activity. It is an expressive and creative tool through which children can share ideas they truly care about. The environment reflects the image of the child as a capable learner in the ways in which it is organized, materials are made accessible, and documentation of learning is visible throughout (Wein 2014; Wurm 2005).

> **The hundred languages of children:** Play is valued as the most effective way young children learn. In explorations children are invited to use hundreds of "languages" that represent the diverse ways they explore, think, discover, and communicate their observations and theories about the world around them. In our classroom, I have noticed that these languages are process-based and include drawing, painting, sculpting, constructing, dancing, and even beading. Most of the time, the process (or action) of learning is more important than the product (or artifact). Children are encouraged to revisit and refine their understandings through multiple attempts and representations of these ideas over time. Learning is cyclical and organic rather than a traditional linear progression (Wein 2014; Wurm 2005).

> **Relationships with families and the community:** Family is very important, and a community approach to child raising is embraced by many who appreciate the Reggio Emilia approach. Families exist as advocates for their children and are considered a vital component of a successful school environment. They are welcomed into the classroom as they share expertise, resources, knowledge, and support, and their ideas, opinions, and experiences help shape curriculum and policy. School is considered the focal point in the community, and families are welcomed to provide the best experience possible for all children (Wein 2014; Wurm 2005).

> **The role of teachers:** In Reggio Emilia, educators are considered guides in the classroom, listening to children's observations and questions and supporting emerging interests by scaffolding classroom experiences. Attuned and reflexive educators carefully observe and document children's activities. Educators are play partners and researchers, uncovering deeper intentions in children's interactions and using these to plan future learning experiences. All adults in the classroom and school work together to ensure

a cohesive approach that values children's explorations and to ensure adequate tools, materials, and experiences can be used to support all children (Wein 2014, 2008; Wurm 2005).

> **Learning through projects and documentation:** Educators actively observe and interact with children as they play and explore together in the classroom. As children express a curiosity or wonder about a topic, educators nurture this spark by providing tools, materials, and activities that help provoke children into deeper exploration. Emergent learning is spontaneous as educators ebb and flow together with children, requiring flexibility in planning and implementation as explorations unfold. Educators work together with small groups of children in these projects, building on previous knowledge and experiences and using available materials to evolve individual and collective understandings. Educator observation and documentation help make children's learning visible and help plan next steps for enhanced learning. Educators often must be responsive and flexible in changing routines and activities, improvising alongside the children while simultaneously planning for future learning opportunities (Wein 2014; Wurm 2005).

The processes involved in computational thinking look very similar to those followed in Reggio Emilia–inspired classrooms that embrace the inquiry process. Consider your classroom:

> Is there a place for the implementation of these ideas in some of your routines?

> What place do student interests have in guiding the direction of activities?

> Can you modify some of your existing lessons to make small changes toward more of an emergent framework?

Recognizing the similarities between the foundations of emergent curriculum and computational thinking is important. Coding has the potential to be used as a language of learning with young children.

## Connecting Reggio Emilia to Computational Thinking

If computational thinking is a problem-solving process, then coding can be thought of as a language or representation of layered student expression. Coding is the action of putting together sequences of instructions and problem-solving if or when the activity does not go as planned. Coding occurs over time as children delve more deeply into further exploring and uncovering their computational ideas in action. Coding empowers children to become computer literate (Umaschi Bers 2018). Coding provides you the freedom to take risks and make mistakes together with your students and to reframe those mistakes through a positive lens! Just as coding provokes deep thinking and venturing into the unknown for children, educators can also enjoy the reprieve from feeling they have to be perfect each moment, and instead embrace messy learning together with the children. Similar to Reggio Emilia's belief that children explore and communicate using hundreds of symbolic languages, coding can exist as language within both computational-thinking situations and emergent-learning contexts. Coding can be both the exploration of a problem and the communication of the response to the problem itself. It transcends disciplines and exists as a flexible language of expression. It is interesting to look at coding through the lens of Reggio Emilia.

If we consider the Reggio image of a child as a coder, we reach several conclusions:

> We recognize that play is the best method of learning for young children. Through play, children can take risks and rehearse for reality, experimenting with different responses to certain situations and learning about themselves and the world around them in safe and supportive environments. They can freely express their emotions and see how their lives intersect with those around them. Children who code can be given opportunities to engage in playful, risk-free coding experiences with multiple entry points.

> We know that children grow and develop over time, strengthening gross- and fine-motor skills as they maneuver their world physically. Big-body coding activities that incorporate physical movement can appeal to kinesthetic learners and incorporate creative actions that appeal to young children. More complex, intricate work can engage the senses and improve fine-motor control.

> We recognize that coding opportunities can build cognitive skills and higher levels of thought as children experience more complex and challenging situations. Various control structures can differentiate the experience and encourage children to think more deeply about the symbolic representation that coding uses. Educators who guide coding activities can modify or challenge based on what they know about that particular child's interests, strengths, needs, and next steps.

> We build the foundation for children's later reading and writing success by exploring language symbolically in coding activities. Symbols that represent ideas within the games can be read, shared, revised, and manipulated, and children can strengthen many aspects of their oral language abilities through the various roles they play. Providing clear directions, transcribing

these into various stable representations (symbolic, written), and engaging in active, responsive listening all ensure a successful coding experience.

> We develop children's social skills as they negotiate, cooperate, take turns, and play by socially constructed rules in structured and open-ended coding games.

> We honor a child as a capable coder by providing time, resources, and support to encourage them to build their own understandings through self-guided projects, being observant and responsive to their needs, and scaffolding and supporting along the way.

> We advocate for children to be producers and not just consumers of information and technology.

> We support children to share their coding knowledge beyond the walls of the classroom to inspire societal change regarding preconceived views of what young children are capable of achieving, and to encourage the positive use of unplugged technology in the classroom.

A Reggio Emilia–inspired environment supports computational activities in several ways:

> by existing as a safe and supportive space where learners can take risks in their coding activities and use mistakes as learning opportunities for refining their work

> by reflecting the children in the classroom so they see themselves represented throughout the space—they cocreate learning centers together with educators based on their interests and ideas, and translate these into their coding projects

> by providing authentic and relevant learning materials that relate to children's interests, and that evolve over time to represent the growth and change the children have experienced in their coding work

> by providing an aesthetic environment filled with interesting objects that promote curiosity and wonder and can spark student imagination, leading to rich coding projects

> by incorporating flexible use of time and space that can be altered based on the needs of children and the various tech projects on which they are working

> by ridding itself of rote practices, including the use of worksheets, textbooks, and tests, and embracing unconventional ways of knowing and being

Recognizing that coding can be one of the Reggio Emilia "hundred languages of learning" demonstrates the following:

> Educators recognize that language can be written, read, and used in meaningful contexts by children in nontraditional ways, using many different symbols (such as drawings, arrows, and grids represented in programming games).

> Children can be effective communicators in the roles of programmer and computer, giving and receiving directions in a clear and concise manner.

> Computational thinking is a process, not product, of learning. The final outcome of any coding activity is not necessarily the creation of code but the skills, knowledge, and experience that children have acquired along the way.

> Educators honor the different forms and representations children's learning can take, encouraging them to continue to rewrite their ideas using code until they are as clearly communicated as possible.

> Children and educators value all languages of learning, including code, equally.

Families and the greater community can support computational thinking in these ways:

> recognizing that all children have the right to learn to code, while advocating for equal access to technology for all children

> actively volunteering time and resources to support computational activities in the classroom (such as sharing special interests or talents or inviting children to understand how tech enhances their job)

> researching how to better support technology-based activities at home, especially for those learners who are interested and ready to apply their understanding in new ways (like exploring coding apps)

> modeling and supporting a growth mindset and recognizing children's mistakes as opportunities for learning and growth

> modeling lifelong learning by becoming coders themselves

Reggio-inspired educators who advocate for technology in the classroom display and embrace these qualities:

> They abandon comfortable and familiar teaching practices and instead embrace the journey of transformative progress.

> They trust in themselves, their students, and the process of learning.

> They are comfortable working in the unfamiliar.

> They understand that learning is a team sport and invite their colleagues to join them on the journey.

> They act as guides in the children's explorations, listening to their stories and questions, supporting them with their interests, and scaffolding experiences to explore these wonderings more deeply using the language of technology.

> They are attuned and flexible in their planning and implementation of new coding activities as they observe children within the learning environment and respond to their learning interests and needs.

> They carefully observe and document children in rich moments of computational thinking using a variety of tools and resources (photos, videos, anecdotal notes, transcripts of conversations).

> They make the rich learning that occurs in computational activities visible through the careful collection, organization, representation, and reflection of pedagogical documentation.

> They become coders together with children, engaging in playful and authentic explorations, solving problems, and reflecting on how to improve the experiences moving forward.

> They are trailblazers as they advocate for change in education.

## The Inquiry Process

The inquiry process is a four-step educational approach that empowers children to investigate meaningful questions they have about the world around them. Many unplugged coding activities can follow the inquiry process. In inquiry-based learning, children are encouraged to investigate an area of interest or solve a problem that is of immediate relevance and curiosity to their lives. Educators support children by providing regular opportunities for exploration and reflection using the authentic resources and situations of daily classroom life. As children explore, educators weave curriculum and assessment opportunities throughout the experiences to fulfill their mandates and stay true to the intentions of the inquiry. This is a very different approach than that taken by those who are more comfortable with traditional educational practices. Educators and children assume various roles in the experience—observing a problem, gathering information, supporting one another, experimenting with different solutions, and communicating their findings to a greater audience. The inquiry process may differ from classroom to classroom but usually follows the same problem-solving format used in traditional mathematical approach (Heick 2019).

The first step of an inquiry project is often sparked by an authentic student question, need, curiosity, or teacher-provided invitation or challenge. This may be related to wonderings that have emerged in free-choice activity time or the result of a problem or question that occurred in routine daily activities. Children use many questions to help them refine their inquiry and narrow the scope of their exploration.

Once a topic of exploration has emerged, children use their existing knowledge and experience with the given topic to better reflect on what they already know and have experienced regarding their topic or problem of exploration. In this next step, they can revise their original question if needed or decompose it into smaller, more manageable parts to explore. Using a wealth of information, including classroom resources and the educator as a guide, children can design a plan for how to move forward in their explorations. They can simultaneously consult other sources of information for support and guidance and continually refine their focus to ensure they are on track in their explorations.

In the third step of the inquiry process, children put their plans into action and test their ideas. As they work, they gather observations and information about the progress of their research along the way. Children can revisit their plans and alter the direction of their work, gathering new resources and sources of information as needed. Children can monitor their progress to ensure they are on track in implementing their plans. At the conclusion of their work, they can gather, organize, and interpret their findings.

In the final step of the inquiry process, children can reflect on the inquiry journey they've taken and arrive at a final conclusion. It's important to share new knowledge and understanding with others, and children can determine the most effective venue for doing so. Reflecting on the entire experience is important, and children can use their new knowledge and understanding to inspire future work in some way. Perhaps new questions arose from the inquiry and children want to use these as the next step in their learning.

In this inquiry process, the educator acts as guide, mentor, coresearcher, observer, and documenter. It is a challenging, multifaceted role that requires us to experience many realities together as we support children, gather evidence of their learning, and use our observations to both propel the learning forward and document what we are observing to make it visible. Relinquishing control in the classroom and trusting in a process that we haven't structured from start to finish takes courage. Doing so can be simultaneously thrilling and terrifying. Having courage to venture into the unknown and placing confidence in your abilities as an educator and trust in your students (as well as having a solid understanding of your curriculum and assessment obligations) will give you the support you need to take this journey! Sometimes educators lead; other times we follow.

## Connecting Reggio Emilia and Coding

In this chapter, I have shared information about the Reggio Emilia approach to education, hoping that it will inspire you to consider the role that authentic, emergent practices can have in your classroom. Many similarities exist between the foundations of Reggio Emilia and the benefits of engaging children in regular activities that promote computational thinking in the classroom. Coding can exist as both a language of expression and an authentic child-led activity, inspiring children to create complex representations and realities to explore.

These approaches have deeply guided my practice and shaped who I am today. The context of my classroom and reality is different than yours, and what has worked for me might not work in the same way for you. However, as I read, learn, and grow, I incorporate new ideas along the way. Our classroom and program are a constant work in progress, continuing to evolve and change over time as the children and I learn together. Introducing coding to my students has inspired me to rethink traditional models of education and how complex thinking and problem-solving can be used in innovative ways. Engaging children in daily math and language activities is a responsibility for every teacher. How we do it is what will make the difference. Energizing, engaging, exciting unplugged coding activities may be the catalyst needed to ignite that spark of passion and cultivate the growth mindset that each child deserves.

In the remaining chapters of this book, I hope to inspire you to rethink your teaching practice and consider how coding can enhance the educational program you offer children. The activities are presented in a simple and easy-to-understand format, suitable for all experience levels. Activities are frameworks and can be modified based on the interests, strengths, and needs of your students, and the context of the inquiries you are exploring. You may find that working from the beginning of the book is helpful if you or your students are coding novices. Or you may prefer to skip ahead and try different activities as interests emerge in your classroom. As you try new activities, become an empowered producer of knowledge and share your ideas beyond your classroom walls! You know your students best. What matters most is taking a chance, moving a little outside your comfort zone, becoming a colearner, reframing mistakes as opportunities, embracing success, and celebrating your achievements with others. It's a tall order, but if you can do all of that, you are well on your way to becoming a master coder!

## CHAPTER 3

# Introducing and Manipulating the Coding Board

*Quinn rushed off the bus, clutching a drawing in his hand. He couldn't get to me fast enough and almost missed the last step.*

*"Mama! I made a computer game! Look!" And sure enough, there in his hand was a drawing of what appeared to be a screen with a keyboard below.*

*"Tell me about your game!" I encouraged him.*

*Quinn proceeded to describe a rich, detailed story about a hero escaping a bad guy, running and jumping through a labyrinth of mazes and tunnels on the "screen" to get to the treasure chest first. As he told his story, he used his finger to trace the actions of the figure through his drawing.*

*"How does it work?" I wondered.*

*"Oh, that I don't really know," he said as he shrugged his shoulders. "This is just pretend. I don't know how to make it a game in real life. I wish I could though—that would be exciting!"*

What image do you have of the learner in your classroom? In Reggio Emilia–inspired spaces, children are viewed as curious and capable members of a democratic learning environment where they explore and create rich and complex understandings of the world around them. Educators who embrace this view recognize that children come to school with a wealth of previous experiences and ideas, and they are driven by their desire to learn and grow. Each child is unique and provided the individual time, space, and resources he or she needs to be successful.

In the example I shared above, it is clear that Quinn is a curious and creative child, representing his previous experiences with imaginative games through the language of drawing. He understands many components of his story, including the setting, characters, and plot, but is not sure how to use a program to animate his ideas into a game. Reflect for a minute and consider what you think would be an effective next step to better support him in this interest. If Quinn was your student, how might you use his interests in stories and games to plan rich next steps for his learning? Most educators might default to incorporating reading and writing into Quinn's experiences: read him storybooks about games, ask him to write sentences to correspond with his picture, or introduce him to new words to help build his vocabulary. Now that I code regularly with children, I look at their work in a different way. Quinn's drawing reminds me of the mapping experiences referred to earlier in the book. His picture is a story map, representing a place and time where something has happened. Helping Quinn transfer his knowledge onto an unplugged coding board would be a meaningful next step to better support his interests, animate his character to retell his story, and extend his learning into better understanding how programmers can code stories on a computer.

A child points at a part of his picture while explaining what his drawing represents.

## Coding Basics

Before we become proficient with any new activity, we must first become comfortable and familiar with the basics—the materials needed, common terminology, design of the process or activity, rules that structure the experience, and ways in which we can manipulate them to our advantage. This is especially important for educators who are new to coding. We want to feel comfortable enough within the parameters of the activity that we can support children and scaffold based on their interests and needs. We don't need to be experts, but we do need to be knowledgeable enough to feel comfortable in our work. We can grow together with the children as we delve more deeply into computational thinking. Reggio-inspired educators who view children as competent in their own explorations provide challenging tools and materials to use freely and in thoughtfully guided explorations. Consider your own experiences when learning something new. For example, when first learning to ride a bike, there are many things we must learn how to use (brakes, gears, spokes, pedals, wheels), but understanding that riding a bike is all about being balanced in movement is important too. With patience and lots of practice, a person will become familiar and comfortable with riding, perhaps eventually venturing off the road and onto more challenging terrain, such as wooded trails and bike parks. We can look at learning to code in the same way.

In this book, I will share dozens of coding games and activities that I have explored throughout the years. Some have been teacher initiated, newly presented to the children for their consideration and involvement, and others have been in direct response to an expressed question or interest the children might have had. Regardless of the spark for the activity, the format for engaging children in each coding lesson has remained the same. The basic format for each activity incorporates what I know about best practices from three-part math lessons, while infusing whole-group activities with information observed and documented from free-choice activities. Each activity includes preparation work, a "minds-on" warm-up, main "working on it" lesson, and practice and consolidation.

Before beginning a lesson, I gather the corresponding materials. I consider what prior knowledge and experience children might have had with the concepts and anticipate what curriculum and assessment opportunities the activities might fulfill.

As the first part of our lesson, I introduce key vocabulary to the children in the form of a minds-on warmup. I explain the different materials needed for the lesson and invite them to participate in an open-ended activity that sparks their interest and helps set the stage for the following activity. This sometimes involves sharing a relevant book or video, referring to a previous experience, or asking a question or issuing a small challenge for children to work on independently or in pairs.

In the middle of the block of time, the children are engaged in a main programming activity that is modeled to the whole group (which I refer to as a "working on it" lesson) and then practiced in a variety of ways (whole group, pairs, and so forth). Connections are made to children's previous experiences and ideas, and any relevant information from the minds-on activity is woven within. In this time, the children incorporate relevant terminology into their explanations and are supported directly in their explorations by an educator and their peers.

Children are then able to use the ideas and activities explored during the lesson in subsequent play experiences and centers throughout the day. This provides additional time for them to practice, explore, experiment, and share their work with others and use the coding activities to support their own ideas. At the end of our day, we gather again for a practice and consolidation circle, where children are invited to share their learning and reflect on their experiences with peers in a whole group. Any questions or concerns that the children might have experienced in their coding activities, including problems with their code or challenges they need help with, are brought to the attention of the whole group during this time. I attempt to weave the children's observations and experiences back to our initial lesson or activity and ask for their suggestions for how we might move forward. After the lesson, I record key observations I have made regarding the children's work, "back map" the experience to see what additional curriculum expectations we might have fulfilled that I did not initially anticipate, and plan for the next lesson or activity to move children's thinking forward.

Throughout the entire coding lesson and subsequent activities, I use observation and documentation to help me gather relevant and important information to assess the children's experiences, better understand their learning, and plan for future coding work. Documentation is complex; it refers to the process of gathering evidence and artifacts from the children to honor their experiences and make the learning visible to families, administration, and colleagues (Wein 2008, 2014). Through the process of documentation, educators can make connections between events, reflecting on previous coding work and planning ahead to future programming opportunities. I have found that in coding experiences, there are many ways to successfully gather, analyze, and share various forms of documentation. Photos and videos can help showcase the collaboration and complex creations that children invent and use in their play. Recorded or written transcripts of their conversations can demonstrate the communication and problem-solving that they have used throughout. Interviews with children can provide detailed answers to specific questions an educator might have about a child's design process, and teacher narrative and reflection can help piece together various artifacts of learning. In our classroom, we have collected and displayed documentation on bulletin boards, in individual student portfolios, through learning stories, and in the various communiqués we share on social media. Sharing documentation beyond the classroom helps others connect with our coding journey, keeps families informed as to what their children are learning at school, and empowers children as producers of information as they contribute to the global experience of using coding in the classroom.

## Introducing the Coding Board

Regardless of whether the coding begins in your classroom as a teacher-provided invitation for learning (you suggest it to children), or in response to a child's wondering (they suggest it to you as an activity to explore), providing time for the children to become comfortable with the materials needed, fluent in the common terminology used, and well grounded in the basic rules is important for their subsequent success. In our classroom, the majority of our early coding experiences used a coding board, representing the metaphorical hardware of a computer, used for the specific purpose of helping us engage in coding activities.

A coding board helps children practice the concept of relative location, or how the location of an object on the board can be described by its relation to something else. The board also helps children practice representing their ideas in different ways. Our board was created by placing masking tape in a grid formation on top of a large piece of recycled plexiglass. Others have easily created grids by marking them on the carpet or tabletop, using masking tape (to create really large grids), drawing grids using permanent markers on clear shower curtains or tablecloths (easy to transport to other areas of the school, such as the hallway or outdoors), painting waterproof lines on outdoor surfaces, or using recycled checkerboards (to add variety and interest). Regardless of how you prepare your grid, the important aspect is that it is big enough for all the children to see and use. Young children are eager to learn about the world around them through physical manipulation. Free exploration with the coding board is important because children need time to manipulate objects and incorporate their previous spatial-reasoning experiences and ideas into new experiences to reach more evolved understandings.

A coding grid and arrow coding cards are the basic materials for many unplugged coding activities.

In addition to the coding board, having loose parts to manipulate within the coding is important. Establishing loose parts as coding characters will engage your children and provide the context for the creation of a story in the initial coding experience. Following the lead of your learners, select materials that are of high interest and storytelling value. In our classroom, we often use convenient loose parts we find in our space, such as cars, dolls, miniature dinosaurs or animals, and even photos of the children glued onto blocks as gaming pieces. I refer to these as "coding characters" because they are the little pieces that become manipulated through story lines on the board. If the coding board is the setting of the story, the loose parts are the characters or players being maneuvered and manipulated within the game. We also use loose parts when adding details to better establish the setting of our coding stories (like green paper grass for a retelling of the "Three Billy Goats Gruff," blue felt water for ocean adventures, or wooden blocks as bridges for mini cars to travel on). These enhancements add interest and variety to our games, enticing children and adding initial "buy-in" factor.

Lastly, establishing the basic rules that govern the game are important for all children so there is a shared understanding of what is happening in the coding experience. It also helps educators work in unfamiliar situations because it provides a baseline from which to begin. In computational thinking, *representation* is how computers store and manipulate data. In early coding experiences, children can represent ideas on the coding board, using symbols, such as arrows, and these symbols represent some type of action.

Establishing common rules is important too. The arrow can indicate direction, and the number of arrows in total can represent how many moves in that direction a player is going to use. With experience, children can innovate their own coding directions and determine the representations for each so that there is communal understanding of the new "language."

## Basic Coding Games

Included below are basic games that help children become comfortable with the hardware, language, and rules used in basic unplugged coding games. In each activity, I will discuss the materials needed, instructions for how children play, and suggestions for what observations educators might use to assess learning. These descriptions are short and easy to understand and implement. While you read, consider what role they might play in your classroom; how you can modify the activities to better meet the interests, strengths, and needs of your learners; and how they relate to your curriculum obligations. Consider how these activities complement other curriculum areas of your classroom programming (such as literacy, math, and art). When selecting the story for your games (setting, characters, or plot), reflect on how you might use the children's current interests or favorite read-alouds as inspiration for your unplugged coding work.

## Hardware-Free Exploration

**Materials:** coding grid, loose parts to manipulate, arrow coding cards

**Instructions:** Provide time for the children to freely explore the materials to stimulate causal thinking about their relationships. Place the grid in a space where a number of children have easy access, and provide the loose parts and arrow coding cards sorted in separate baskets. The children may incorporate previous experiences with mapping and gaming, including moving characters around the grid or placing arrows to record the path they have taken or are about to take. Some children may use the grid as a graphic organizer to sort arrows in rows by direction. Others may randomly fill the area of the grid with cards and loose parts or create patterns within the squares. Observe the children to determine their previous experiences with the materials, see how they are already using them, and collect any questions or wonderings they might have.

A child manipulates a character he has created on the coding board during free exploration.

Use open-ended questioning in your interactions to better understand why the children are manipulating the materials in these ways. Incorporate math terminology whenever possible ("I see you are placing the arrows in a horizontal line" or "You are sorting the cards because they all share a similar characteristic"). Model use of the materials by placing the loose parts in different areas of the grid and showing the path of movement they can take by placing arrows in the grid squares. These observations can guide your work and help inform future opportunities.

**Observations:** Are the children interested in the activity and materials? Are they working collaboratively or independently? Are stories emerging in their play? What math and language behaviors are you seeing? Can you use some of the play as prompts for the next whole-group discussion? Do the children appear to need more time to freely explore the materials, or do they seem ready and eager to move on to a more organized coding format?

**Next Steps:** Consider the readiness of the children and whether or not introducing a more formal coding activity at the next whole-group time would be a sensible next step. If so, plan for what the context of the coding activity might be. A current interest? A favorite read-aloud? Gather the materials and prepare how you will hook the children into the experience and spark their curiosity. ■

As children become comfortable with the coding materials, educators can plan the next whole-group activity to help children shape the experience and make the connection that coding involves creating a sequence that communicates an instruction or action for another person (or computer) to follow. Reference the free-play exploration that children had when first exploring the grid, and show photos to punctuate your points if applicable. In your whole-group conversation, highlight that although there were many rich ideas happening on the board, it was difficult to understand the direction of the play without some type of order or rule. Real-world experiences, like the actions on a coding board, can be represented in a specific way so they are understood by all users. Explain to children that an **algorithm** is a series of steps or actions taken in sequence to achieve an end result or goal. Algorithms can be long or short, depending on the coder's preference. Sometimes the number of steps aren't important in the context of the game being played, but at other times they are (like when finding that the fastest or most efficient path wins the game). When children give step-by-step directions to move an object on the coding board, they are communicating in algorithms. Educators can use the coding board, loose parts, and arrow cards to demonstrate to the children that the paths taken by characters on the grid can be represented in these sequences, or algorithms.

## Introducing Algorithms

**Materials:** coding grid, loose parts to manipulate, arrow coding cards

**Instructions:** Establish an engaging story line together with the children. Perhaps a recent inquiry or read-aloud can be used as inspiration to guide the activity. In our classroom, one of the first coding stories the children created was for moving a trick-or-treater from house to house on Halloween—a highly motivating experience to which they could all relate. Determine a starting point to indicate the beginning of the coding path and an ending point where a character will stop. Explain that moves are horizontal or vertical on the grid (not diagonal), and allow only one move per square. Encourage children to analyze the grid for possible paths that the character might take. As the children articulate their ideas, represent what they are saying by placing an arrow in each spot on the grid.

Continue to place arrows on the grid until the entire path is clearly outlined. Using the cards as a guide, hold the character piece in your hand and manipulate it through the path, clearly touching each spot on the grid by jumping it from square to square. Do not deviate from the path. As you jump, explain aloud to the children that you are following the established path and moving your character from start to finish. Once the path is complete, clear the arrows, determine new starting and ending points, and encourage the children to create a new way for the character to arrive at the end spot.

A coding path is created, leading the animal to the food.

**Observations:** Are the children interested in the activity? Do they seem engaged and invested in the experience even when it is not their turn to manipulate the materials? What questions are they asking about the game? Do they have ideas for how to extend or enhance the experience? What do the children do with the materials when an adult is not supervising the center?

**Next Steps:** Place the materials at a center for the children to explore during guided centers or times where they can self-select their activities. Observe their interactions and note how they are using the coding materials and interacting with one another while telling a story in code or solving problems when they arise. Consider how to incorporate your observations into subsequent activities. ■

As children become comfortable manipulating characters on the coding board, their understanding of the representation of the coding sequence using arrow coding cards will increase. Providing opportunities for children to see and understand that coding language doesn't always have to be embedded directly into the grid will help them internalize this new language. One way to do this is by removing the algorithm from the grid and recording it in different ways. This helps set the stage for sharing programming language in formats that can be shared and understood beyond the classroom.

## Reading and Writing Algorithms

**Materials:** coding grid, loose parts to manipulate, arrow coding cards, paper, markers

**Instructions:** In a similar fashion to the previous activity, encourage the children to establish the context for the coding game, including a familiar setting, characters, and story line to follow. Determine the start and end locations. Model for them the path that the character can take to move from the start to the finish location. Instead of placing the arrow cards directly on the grid, place them in sequence next to the grid. Similar cards can be lined together. For example, instead of writing the algorithm by placing the cards in one line (*forward, forward, right, right, right, forward*), create lines of code that group similar directions together (first row reads *forward, forward*; second row reads *right, right, right*). Once the children become proficient with reading the lined code isolated from the board, present the code first and then challenge the children to read it and move their character based on what they see represented in the algorithm.

This type of representation empowers the children to record their code using representational, written language that can be followed by another user.

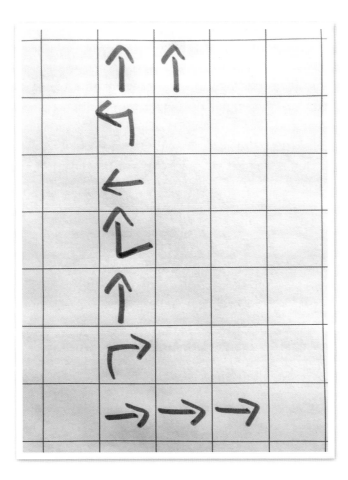

*Coding directions can be recorded as arrows and read by children separately from the coding board.*

Instead of orally explaining the code their characters must take to move on the board, they can create a permanent representation that can be read and used by another person. Children who cannot yet draw arrows (it's surprisingly difficult for many young children to do) can manipulate sticky notes with predrawn arrows or use arrow cutouts created by an adult ahead of time.

**Observations:** Do the children seem to understand that the steps taken on the coding grid can be symbolically represented with arrow cards? If they are drawing the arrows, are they able to do so effectively and with control so that one can tell their direction? Are the children interested in recording the coding path in this manner, or do they have different ideas? Can the children translate written words to code and vice versa?

**Next Steps:** Offer materials in a small-group activity during free-choice time. Encourage the children to continue creating their own coding paths and representing directions using arrow coding cards placed in the correct sequence. Alternately, offering coding sequences first and encouraging them to follow the sequence with loose parts on the grid might also help turn this abstract concept into something easier to see and understand. ■

I found that with practice children were quite keen to keep a permanent record of their paths. This was especially true for stories they were emotionally invested in or wanted to enact in real life. One easy way to do this was by providing smaller coding grids that they could manipulate and write on directly. Paper activities appealed to various learning styles and helped the children create a lasting record of the coding experience that they could take home and share with families. These were also suitable artifacts to add to documentation displays around the classroom (along with photos, narratives, transcripts of conversation, and other items) to make the deep learning visible to outsiders.

## Grid-Paper Coding

**Materials:** photocopied grid paper (the size of the squares is dependent on your group, can be large or small), writing materials

**Instructions:** In a similar fashion to the previous coding experiences, encourage the children to create a story line for their code. They can choose a starting and ending point on their grid and mark these accordingly. Designating the starting point green and the ending point red might be a helpful visual cue. The children

The green dot indicates the starting point for the coding path. The red dot is the ending point. Directional arrows are drawn in each square, showing the path from green to red.

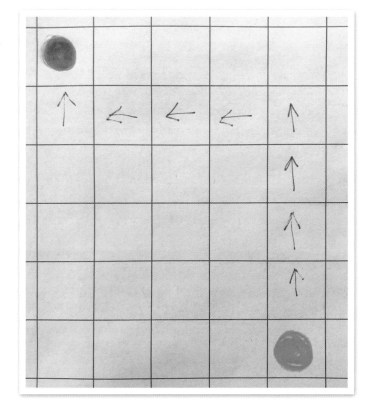

can plan out the path by analyzing the different ways to move from start to finish. Using a pencil or marker, the child can then code the path a character might take by drawing arrows directly in each grid square. These can be written in arrow code underneath to help articulate the moves needed to be taken from start to finish.

**Observations:** Can the children transfer the experiences they had with the hardware coding grid to symbolic grid-paper activities? Is the size of the grid (both the paper and individual squares) appropriate for their interests and needs? Should the grid be differentiated in some way? What other materials are the children incorporating into their grid coding? What else would the children like to do with the coding grid? Are the children interested in transferring activities from the hardware grid to paper grids?

**Next Steps:** Offer a variety of grids for the children to use. Ask them for suggestions on what might enhance their experience or promote the stories they are portraying on the grids (stickers, different colors, and so on). Consider offering a giant paper grid in a large open area and asking the children to work on a collaborative paper grid all together. Paper grids can also be sent home for families to use as a "home connection" to better support the work happening at school and invite them into better understanding coding work with their children. Incorporate grids into other areas of the school, including the outdoors, and encourage children to use them to record their stories. ■

I noticed over time that although children developed a quick understanding of how to manipulate characters on the grid, they were using the words *up* and *down* to describe a character's movements, which wasn't necessarily accurate. When a character is moved, the language used to indicate direction is relative to that particular character's perspective. What may appear to be an up or down movement to us may not necessarily be accurate positional language for that character—it would be better to use *forward* and *backward*. I also found the terms *up* and *down* misleading because they indicate a vertical movement, and the two-dimensional coding boards we were using were horizontal.

Books are a wonderful way to engage children emotionally in an activity. Rich and detailed illustrations can help children use spatial skills to understand the pictures, and educators can engage children in rich discussions to share previous experiences and make connections, promoting a deeper understanding of perspective. Books can also encourage the use of positional language in a specific context, helping children connect oral language to an illustration and practice using it in a meaningful context before applying it in advanced coding on the board. This also reinforces perspective.

## Introducing Perspective

**Materials:** books that encourage perspective taking, including *Yellow Ball* (Molly Bang); *Up, Down, and Around* (Katherine Ayres and Nadine Bernard Westcott); *Rosie's Walk* (Pat Hutchins); *Big Bug* (Henry Cole); *You Are (Not) Small* (Anna Kang and Christopher Weyant) and *Flotsam* (David Wiesner)

**Instructions:** Spend time exploring each book based on the interests and needs of your group. As you read the story aloud, encourage the children to observe the illustrations in depth. Use think-alouds to share your own observations, and encourage the children to discuss what they see and think for each picture in the story. Use positional language as it relates to the character's perspective to describe what is happening on each page. Ask the children to consider the perspective of the characters and their own interpretations as they carefully examine the story line and illustrations. Encourage the children to make connections to their experiences when guiding characters in subsequent activities using a coding board. Help them make the connection that a character is being moved based on its location in relation to other objects when coding on the board. Sometimes considering a bird's-eye view can be helpful when planning a path. Place props that can represent the story's characters in your sensory tables. Encourage the children to retell the story using the props and to practice using positional language in their interactions with others.

**Observations:** Are the books engaging for the children? Do the children use the illustrations effectively to help support their comprehension? Can they use positional language in the correct context when discussing what they see and hear in each story? What connections to their own lives do they make in their conversations? What ideas do they have for using the books in subsequent activities?

**Next Steps:** Consider placing the books in your classroom library for further reading and exploration. Some books can be used to enhance sensory bins and promote dramatic role playing and exploration (such as placing loose parts to represent the characters and setting from a book in the sand or water table). Encourage the children to retell and innovate the texts with loose parts. Books can also be placed at the writing center and used as mentor texts as the children refer to them for inspiration to author and illustrate their own stories. ∎

Once the children are comfortable with creating and representing coding paths using algorithms, they can be challenged to manipulate characters in strategic ways, enhancing their design process, which is the series of steps taken to solve a specific problem. Introducing obstacles on the board can be a fun and challenging way to encourage more complex problem-solving. Obstacles are blockages that prevent a character from using a specific square on the grid. In a Halloween coding game, children placed scary objects, including plastic spiders and bats, into squares the characters could not use. When coding on grid paper, the children depicted obstacles by crossing out squares that could not be used in the coding paths. Introduce obstacles slowly to the children—one or two on the board at a time—so that they can strategize how to maneuver around and still successfully reach their destination. Once they are confident in their abilities, place obstacles to totally block off a path and ask them how to problem solve to manipulate their characters. When posing this challenge, my students suggested creating a new coding card that represented a "jump" action so the characters could jump over any obstacle in their way. Your children may have other ideas for character actions that they'd like to represent and explore (such as fly, leap, catapult, or swing).

## Introducing Obstacles

**Materials:** coding grid, loose parts to manipulate, arrow coding cards, obstacles (such as wooden blocks or rocks), paper, markers

**Instructions:** Establish a story with a setting and characters. After establishing your starting and ending places, block off certain parts of the coding grid with obstacles. These spaces are no longer usable by the character and cannot be included in the algorithm. Encourage the children to plan out their path, either by placing arrow cards directly on the coding grid if needed or next to the

Obstacles are placed on the grid for the animal to maneuver around while traveling to the food.

coding grid. Depending on the difficulty of the board, encourage the children to maneuver their characters safely around the obstacles until they successfully reach the end position. When the children are ready, challenge them by blocking off an entire section of the grid with obstacles, making it impossible for the character to proceed. Ask them to consider their design process and problem solve how to finish the path. As they introduce new character actions (jump, fly, hop), encourage them to represent these symbolically and draw them on blank coding cards. For example, when introducing the "jump" action, my students used a double arrow as the symbol for the code. Any new actions created in the obstacle challenges are now part of the children's programming repertoire and can be used in future activities.

**Observations:** Do the children comprehend the idea of an obstacle? Can they problem solve when one or multiple obstacles are blocking a direct path? How do they respond to and cope with challenging situations? What strategies do the children use when they become stuck? Are they interested in creating complex movements for characters to use, or do they deviate to an easier response?

**Next Steps:** Encourage the children to create a list of verbs that characters on the coding board might use and design symbols that correspond to each one. These can then be drawn on coding cards and used as universal symbols in future activities. ■

As children become proficient with designing algorithms, they will want to become more efficient in how they write their codes. A control structure is a block of programming that analyzes variables and choses a direction within the code based on the specified parameters. Control structures help determine the order in which instructions are followed within an algorithm and can be helpful for children to consider when playing with the sequence and efficiency of their code. **Optimization** helps children consider the most efficient way to solve a problem (such as the fewest number of steps or most logical path to take). For example, if a child has a sequence that they want to repeat a certain number of times, they can write it fully or use a loop to make the code more advanced and efficient. Loops are repeated patterns of instructions to be followed in an algorithm. On our coding board, the children wanted the mama cat to run three times around a mean dog before escaping it. Writing that amount of code would take a long time and open the children to more possibility for making mistakes in the directions. I found looping to be an abstract concept for my students to grasp at first, and it took repeated practice (no pun intended) for them to use it effectively. Helping children identify the core of a pattern and then consider how looping it makes it easier for a user or computer to understand will benefit them in the future.

## Looping Beads

**Materials:** enticing loose parts such as beads or gems, six-inch sections of string or yarn

**Instructions:** Model for the children how the loose parts can be arranged in a simple or complex repeating pattern (depending on the needs of your students). Discuss the pattern and encourage the children to identify its core. Take one piece of yarn and create a circular loop around the core, identifying it for students. Continue to loop more yarn around the remaining cores until everything has been segmented. Encourage the children to count how many loops are contained within the one repeating pattern. Explain to the children that loops can also be included in algorithms in a similar way. Provide each child (or pair) with a collection of loose parts and yarn, and encourage them to create a repeating pattern and loop around the core using the yarn.

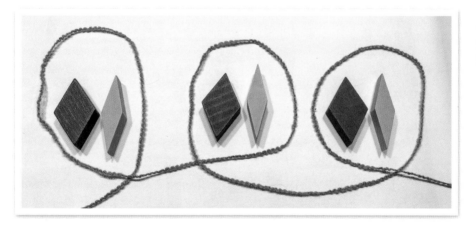

The core of the pattern is isolated and identified by loops of string.

**Observations:** Can the children extend patterns created by an adult or peer? Are they able to independently create their own patterns? Can they orally articulate what it is they see? Are their patterns simple or complex in nature? Can the children identify the core of their pattern and those of their peers? Are they able to separate the core and show loops in their entire design? If just the core is provided, can they extend the pattern? Where else can the children notice and name patterns in the world around them?

**Next Steps:** Take photos of the children's patterns. Laminate these and place them together with dry-erase markers in a looping center. Encourage the children to explore one another's patterns and circle the loops. Provide loose parts along with string or yarn, and the children can continue to create and explore increasingly more-complex patterns. ■

## Loopy Exercise Lines

**Materials:** pocket chart, number cards, action cards (such as *clap, jump, toe touch, push up*)

**Instructions:** Display the pocket chart in an area where children have lots of personal space to move about. Introduce the activity by reminding the children that when we code, we create algorithms to outline a sequence of activities. In this activity, children are going to be writing code for a series of exercises they will then perform. Model the activity by placing action cards in the pocket chart. Use only one type of action per line. Ask the children to perform a specific number of each action in a loop (for example, first row displays five jump cards, second row displays seven toe-touch cards, third row displays ten high knees). Once the exercise code is written, lead the children through the series of exercises from start to finish. It might be helpful to have a child leading the group, pointing to each action in the pocket chart as it is performed.

Exercise action cards are displayed in a pocket chart for children to follow.

**Observations:** Are the children interested in the activity? Can they follow the sequence of exercises effectively? Do they understand the concept of looping, and are they able to repeat the activities in the correct sequence? Can the children create increasingly more complex loops? What is their response when they make mistakes in their loops?

**Next Steps:** Designate an open area in the classroom or outside yard for continued exploration with the exercise cards. Children can continue to create their own sequence of movements and lead one another through various routines to further practice the concept of looping, using kinesthetic, big-body movements. Consider adding music or props (like colorful scarves or instruments) to enhance the experience. ■

Loops are an effective way to help children think about patterns in complex ways. Once the children become comfortable with the concept, group various actions into a loop and encourage them to follow the code. Children can transfer their knowledge of loops to coding boards and represent the number of spaces that need to be moved in a certain direction using a number card next to an arrow.

This code

can be represented as this loop.

Exercise Loops

**Materials:** variety of exercise cards, tape, chart paper, markers

**Instructions:** In this activity, children will again follow an exercise code that incorporates patterns, but this time the pattern's core will be represented in a loop and will use different exercises. For example, the loop might be clap, jump, toe touch. Determine what exercises are going to be in the first loop, and tape them together in a row on the paper. Draw a circle around all to indicate they are going to be in a loop together, then identify how many times the loop is going to be repeated by writing a number next to it. Help the children practice one loop at first by acting out the exercises written together in the code. For example, if the loop was written 5 (clap, jump, toe touch), then the action would be repeated five times. Once the children appear comfortable with how loops work, encourage them to create multiple lines of exercise code and loop them in a specific number of ways. Challenge them to create many different lines of code and act them out by performing the exercises in the specific order and number of sets as represented by the code. Using a child as a guide, pointing to the code as it's written to help prompt exercisers along in the sequences, might be a helpful visual for children to follow.

Exercise action cards are displayed in a loop for the children to follow.

**Observations:** Is the activity engaging for the children? Are they transferring their understanding of loops to the symbolic code and performing the correct number of exercises in each line? What other suggestions do they have for how the cards can be used? Are they incorporating their growing understanding of looping into other activities?

**Next Steps:** Continue to provide opportunities for the children to explore more complex looping in independent activities during free-choice time. They can continue to create their own sequence of movements and lead one another through various routines to practice the concept of looping further using kinesthetic, big-body movements in an open classroom center, in the gym, or during outside time. Consider inviting another class to join you, and teach them how to follow the loops. ∎

## Embracing Mistakes

In my teaching practice, I promote a growth mindset, and part of this has been embracing and reframing mistakes as opportunities for learning. **Debugging** code is when we analyze what we have written using a sequential and step-by-step analysis (Umaschi Bers 2018). It's helpful for discovering where a problem is when a code doesn't work or anticipating where a potential problem might be before it actually occurs. The children once spent a large block of time writing an intricate code. When they were ready to reveal it to me, there was an unforeseen error in the middle, and the sequence did not work out as expected. They were quite upset and embarrassed. I assured them that errors in code are a normal part of the design process, and we worked together to find and fix the problem in their sequence. Debugging is reminiscent of the Reggio Emilia belief that the classroom is a safe and supportive space where mistakes are perfectly okay and children are free to take risks without fear of failure or regret. It engages children actively in the collaborative problem-solving process and is applicable to many other situations in life when troubleshooting is necessary. I have found that introducing debugging to children encourages them to take greater risks in their coding activities. I use every chance I can to model mistake making and "mistake learning" for children to embed debugging daily into our work and create a culture that reframes errors as opportunities. Children now refer to any error they make as a "bug" and know that they always have a chance to fix the problem and make it better.

### What's Wrong with My Pattern?

**Materials:** variety of loose parts, including buttons, caps, gems, or blocks

**Instructions:** Create a pattern using the loose parts in front of the children. Start with a simple pattern at first and increase the complexity of the patterns you create as the children gain practice and confidence. Purposely include an error in your pattern and ask the children to help you "debug" it by finding the error and fixing it. Create multiple patterns with errors to be debugged, giving children practice finding and fixing problems.

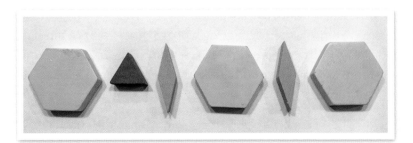

An error is purposely included in this pattern to encourage children to debug it.

**Observations:** Can the children identify the repetition in the pattern? Do they easily notice mistakes? What happens if you incorporate multiple errors in the same pattern? Can children easily identify the core and debug the mistakes? Are the children able to create their own patterns with purposeful errors?

**Next Steps:** Provide time for the children to explore this concept together in a guided activity. Pair children together with a large selection of enticing loose parts. Each child can take turns in the role of pattern coder or debugger. Multiple patterns with errors can be created and fixed, and children can take turns experiencing both roles. Bring the children back together as a whole group to share their experiences and reflect on their understandings in a collaborative conversation. ■

## What's Wrong with My Code?

**Materials:** coding grid, loose parts to manipulate, arrow coding cards

**Instructions:** Establish a story line with the children and select a start and end point for the character's path. Model the activity for the children by stating aloud the path you are coding for the character to travel. Record the algorithm by placing coding cards next to the grid. Purposely make a mistake in the algorithm by placing a card in incorrect sequence. If the children notice, highlight that they debugged your code and prevented a problem. If they do not notice, finish the code and attempt to travel through the path by following it. If the children still do not notice the error, use the opportunity to think aloud that something doesn't seem right while working with the code. You can use the prompts "What happened?" and "What was supposed to happen?" to steer the conversation. Help the children identify the bug and ask for their help in correcting it. Repeat the activity again with the children taking a lead in the coding role.

**Observations:** Are the children able to follow along with the sequence using the coding cards? Do they notice errors in the code easily? What happens if multiple errors are purposely presented in the same code? How do the children cope with feelings of frustration if they become stuck on a problem? What opportunities for discussing and encouraging growth mindset are present in the activity? Are children extending their debugging work to other areas of the classroom and noticing and reframing mistakes as opportunities for growth? Are they using the term *debugging* when correcting mistakes outside of a coding context?

**Next Steps:** Incorporating books and activities that focus on mistake making and growth mindset might be helpful for providing encouragement and support

An error is purposely presented in the code to encourage debugging.

to children. *One* (Kathryn Otoshi), *The Girl Who Never Made Mistakes* (Mark Pett and Gary Rubinstein), *It's Okay to Make Mistakes* (Todd Parr), and *Ish* (Peter H. Reynolds) are all great choices. Even children who cope well with mistakes will benefit from continued reminders that mistakes are growth opportunities. ■

## Which Code Does Not Belong?

**Materials:** set of premade coding algorithms, coding board, loose parts to manipulate, arrow coding cards

**Instructions:** This activity is more complex and will take some time to prepare before playing. Display two full coding algorithms to children in a pocket chart or use a premade paper like the one depicted in the photo (page 46). Establish a story line. Using the coding board, silently go through the process of creating a coding path similar to the initial activities in this chapter. Establish start and end locations, identify a possible path for the character to move, place coding cards in sequence on or beside the grid, and move the player through the sequence. Ask the children to watch you and consider the algorithms displayed in the pocket chart. Which one has the bug and does not belong? As the children offer their opinions, ask them why the code they selected is wrong. Can they articulate their thinking and describe the incorrect step(s) in the sequence? Remove the materials from the coding board, display two new fully written algorithms, and repeat the activity.

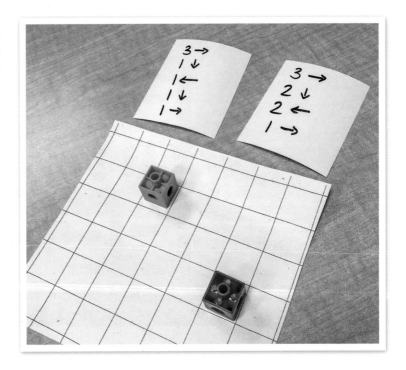

Two sets of code are presented. The children must determine which one is right.

**Observations:** Are the children able to notice the errors in the code and differentiate the differences between the sequencing options? Can they articulate alternative coding paths not presented as options? Do they correct bugs in the codes? Is the activity too easy or too difficult?

**Next Steps:** Encourage the children to create their own versions of this game. They can draw a coding path on a grid and then write various sequences (one correct, many wrong) and challenge their friends to discover the correct code. Laminate children's paths and sequences, and share them in a center with dry-erase markers for other children to explore during free-choice time. Tweet photos of children's coding sequences and invite greater community participation and response to their work. ∎

## Many Ways to Code!

I have implemented computational thinking and unplugged coding into other areas of our program in several ways. These provide differentiated support and encouragement for children and give them additional time to practice coding concepts in a variety of ways.

You can create a coding center in your classroom by adding materials to an existing center, such as the construction area, or creating a new place for children to add materials as they are introduced and used in whole-group situations. In our classroom, we have used the building carpet as our coding area. In addition to the traditional materials already in place in this area (wooden blocks, Legos, large carpet, straws, and connectors), we've added materials over time. Coding arrow cards, blank cards, markers, dry-erase boards, grid paper, different coding grids, a large coding carpet (the learning carpet is a great choice), pocket charts, relevant read-alouds, and any other material children have used in their activities are essential materials. Children can use the center during free-choice time to explore coding activities already presented in whole- and small-group activities or innovate materials by incorporating them into new explorations. For example, one afternoon a group of eager children in my class created a complex construction site where wooden blocks were forming the beams of a skyscraper. They used coding cards as architectural plans to help explain how they were building the structure and referred to these as they worked. If the coding materials were not easily accessible in the area, I'm not sure that the children would have incorporated them as readily into their collaborative building.

Consider creating a rolling coding cart for easy transport to other areas of the school, including the gym, library, and outdoor space. This cart can be stocked with similar materials to those in the coding center, stored in removable baskets for easy use, organization, and cleanup by children. As materials are introduced and used in the classroom, add these to the cart so children can incorporate them into their play. Ask the children to suggest things they think might also enhance their coding play, and incorporate these into future coding experiences. Consider nontraditional ways of embedding coding work into other areas of your school and community.

Invite older children to become **coding buddies** and work together as class partners on a regular basis. Older children can support and scaffold younger children in complex activities, providing them with direct instruction that they may not receive in other classroom work. Paired work provides time for children to engage in rich conversation with more experienced programmers who can act as guides and mentors. Older children can bring their coding experiences into activities and thrive in their mentoring role. They can also share their coding ideas and creations with younger children, providing them a window into future coding possibilities.

Consider preparing extension activities that can be rotated and sent home for children's families to use for a designated length of time. Many families are eager for supplemental materials to be shared between home and school so they can provide extra practice to enhance what children are studying at school. In our classroom, I prepared a number of coding bags that contained versions of the different activities we had been working on during class time. Each bag had an instruction card, relevant materials, and a feedback booklet for family members to communicate to me the experience their family had playing the different games.

These provided a tangible way for families to learn about coding and practice computational thinking in different forms and gave them a way to support their children's interests that differed from traditional homework.

Technology allows the distribution of ideas to a much larger audience than just your classroom or school community. In addition to connecting with families, consider sharing the amazing coding work you are experiencing by reaching out to a greater audience, perhaps building a **personal learning network**, or PLN, on social media. Maybe you can connect virtually with another class and become coding pen pals, sharing your activities and ideas and challenging one another to investigate new problems. In our classroom, we connected with other educators and students by tweeting, blogging, and sharing photos of our activities on social media. Many of these ideas were used and innovated by teachers and children around the world. Their feedback strengthened and refined our learning, and we were inspired to persevere in trying new and more complex ideas and activities because of the rich educational dialogue we were having with other invested coders. You can connect with other like-minded social media users by incorporating related hashtags along with your content (#coding, #kindercoding, #21stedchat, #mathchat, #MTBoS) and building your social media network.

**CHAPTER 4**

# Mindful Makers

*After reading a book about leprechauns, Quinlan and Sage spent time together that day designing and building a trap to leave out in the classroom overnight in hopes of catching one and discovering where he kept his pot of gold.*

> *Quinlan and Sage were busy working at the table, tinkering with loose parts.*
> *"I know, I'll put the cap right here! That way I can sprinkle some sparkles in it to get his attention, and then when he steps in the cap, it will trip this wire and the lid will shut on the box."*
> *"Yes, but what if he doesn't like sparkles? Then he won't go inside."*
> *"What if we set it up so that if someone walks through it from this side, the lid will close or another part of the wall will swing and that will block the door?"*
> *"I'm not sure . . . use duct tape to hold it, and we can test it out first."*
> *After many minutes of experimentation, the children agreed on a design and finalized their project by gluing pieces permanently into place. Motivated by the same goal, the read-aloud had sparked collaborative creation and problem-solving for these young learners.*

## The Kindergarten Environment

Emergent programs embrace inquiry-based learning to guide children's activities in the classroom and beyond. Educators continually support and scaffold the expressed interests of children in the form of open-ended activities and projects. This results in engaged children exploring, discovering, and communicating answers to self-directed questions on a regular basis. They are in control of their learning, and adults are guides on this journey. In the early years, we are encouraging mindfulness in every moment of each day as children tune in to their senses and appreciate moments of pure joy in the classroom. How often have you observed children's enthusiasm for activities, fascination with nature, and resilience in their quest to master a task? Connecting with children and relating to these moments promote a joyful classroom life. As children focus on their senses in explorations—how materials look, feel, smell, sound, and sometimes even taste— they are gathering information to support their inquiries as well as engaging in mindful moments in the classroom.

Early primary classrooms are fluid, evolving environments that continually change over the course of the year, reflecting the children who inhabit them and supporting them in developmentally appropriate activities while integrating learning materials from diverse centers in innovative ways. In Reggio Emilia, the classroom environment is considered the "third teacher" and is continually being shaped by the actions of the children over time (Wein 2008, 2014). Their organization and decor are the public statements that educators share with the rest of the world about their beliefs regarding the image of the child as a learner. Reflect on your surroundings for a moment. What image is evoked when visitors enter and explore your classroom environment? What inspiration do you share for educational journeys and transformations? What message is reflected back to the children in your care? What materials do children have access to, and what are the parameters surrounding their play? Classrooms that contain open-ended tools and materials, time and space to work on self-directed and teacher-provided projects, and rich documentation showcasing the explorations and learning of children present an image of a strong, resilient, and capable learner in a democratic space where all children are considered equal members (Pecaski McLennan 2009; Tarr 2001). Our classroom is multifaceted—a studio, laboratory, and gallery where children can immerse themselves in explorations of wonder and joy. Children are able to create things they truly care about and share these with others. Visitors to our room can review documentation and understand the stories of our learning from the past and see how it informs our practice moving forward. How might you organize your classroom environment and materials and change the routines your children experience through the day to create the same unlimited conditions for learning?

## Our Classroom

Our classroom is a bright and cheerful place where children ebb and flow in a variety of learning centers. I want it to be an aesthetically pleasing space appealing to children's senses, encouraging curiosity and wonder, responding to their needs, and offering continuous possibilities for authentic learning. The room is large and rectangular, with our communal carpet located in the middle and traditional "centers" (including sensory, snack, art, building, and drama) placed in a circular formation around. The image of a web guides me in this design, as I consider each center to be interconnected and related to the others. Children bring materials from different areas to the communal carpet, or a new center, exploring and collaborating with peers in authentic explorations.

Diverse materials from our local community are continually added to our classroom. Children and their families donate interesting objects from their

Our building center offers children many resources and a large area in which to design and create.

homes and yards, and I enjoy sharing treasures that I've found as well. Very few commercial toys and products line our shelves, and the majority of our learning materials are loose parts. Loose parts are found, recycled, and natural materials that can be moved, carried, combined, lined up, repurposed, puzzled together, and taken apart in endless ways. Unlike traditional activities that have predetermined learning goals in mind and are arranged in boxes or bins on shelves, loose parts are not bound by such limits. They come with no specific directions for use; the possibilities are as endless as the children's imaginations. They are cost effective and easy to gather. They are sorted and displayed in clear containers inside the classroom and in the yard. Some loose parts in our room include stones, stumps, pebbles, sea glass, shells, fabric, gems, seedpods, tiles, frames, baskets, and buttons. There is no predetermined end or final product when one is creating with loose parts. They can be sorted, arranged, manipulated, and deconstructed in a variety of ways, integrating rich learning from a number of domains as children control their own activities and explore the world around them using the language of loose parts. One of the most influential projects outlining the beauty and potential for loose parts is described in the book *Beautiful Stuff* (Weisman Topal and Gandini 1999).

Loose parts are essential pieces for inspiring classrooms that encourage making throughout the day. An ideal learning space that supports learning with loose parts is a makerspace. It is a creative area where children can gather to tinker, create, invent, and make connections to their own learning and the world around them. Our classroom exists as a giant makerspace, embracing the constructivist foundations that also inspire Reggio Emilia. In some schools, makerspaces are located in central areas outside of the classroom, including the common entrance or library. Mobile makerspaces can be created and transported to other areas, including the outdoors, by placing baskets of interesting and innovative materials on a rolling cart that can be moved from location to location. In makerspaces children can explore self-directed projects focused on questions or concerns they might have about the world around them or tinker with new and interesting materials to see what develops from their playful explorations. They are able to use a variety of open-ended tools and materials in creative projects. A makerspace is not just a physical place, but is also a "way of being" or educational mindset as children become creators of information and technology and not simply consumers of other people's ideas or products, seeing their creation and knowledge turned into action (Flemming 2015).

Loose parts are integrated into every area of the classroom to encourage tinkering and building with a variety of materials.

## Cultivating a Maker Mindset

Making is more about the culture of learning that is cultivated and nurtured in the classroom than the materials contained within (Fleming 2015). We place an emphasis on the process of creation and problem-solving, and this is valued more in our classroom community than the finished piece or product.

Some classrooms house makerspace centers that offer diverse, open-ended materials for creation. The art studio and construction centers are both examples of makerspaces where children can create permanent and transient pieces using a wealth of loose parts (buttons, caps, blocks, boxes, or tracks). Educators who do not have the space to offer permanent makerspaces might consider designating certain times in their schedules for makerspace activities. "Maker Monday" and "Tinker Tuesday" are common blocks of time set aside specifically for engaging children in open-ended tinkering and making right at the beginning of their school week. Materials can be presented in a common area of the room, including the carpet, and children can be invited to explore self-directed or teacher-initiated projects. This ensures regular access to high-quality materials and large designated blocks of uninterrupted time for student exploration. Benefits of regular making include the following:

> ❯ Children will be encouraged to become explorers as they navigate familiar and new materials in interesting and innovative ways, leading to rich discovery and creation.

> ❯ Children will begin to make connections between objects, experiences, and ideas as they engage in rich problem-solving with an end goal in mind.

> ❯ Children will develop a growth mindset as they experiment and problem solve, using challenges and mistakes as opportunities for change and growth.

> ❯ Children will connect socially and emotionally as they persevere together in complex creation, using one another's perspectives to enhance their projects.

> ❯ Children will become hackers as they modify their designs, use objects differently than their intended purposes, and fuse together ideas from multiple sources.

> ❯ Children will become researchers, solving problems but also generating additional questions for exploration.

## Connecting the Maker Movement to Computational Thinking

In addition to the open-ended option of providing a makerspace in the classroom, we've explored a variety of activities in our classroom that promote a maker mindset while engaging children in computational thinking. As you read each one, consider the **design process** (identify a problem, look for ideas, develop solutions, communicate with others) and how you might be able to integrate or extend the activity into your own educational reality.

The maker movement is about teaching and learning that is focused on student-centered inquiry (Fleming 2015). Today's educational spaces must provide rich and complex spaces for children to use creativity and innovation to solve challenges and investigate areas of great personal interest. Consider your classroom and program, and reflect on whether implementing this is a possibility. Can you make small and steady changes to your environment and schedule that will engage children in regular making? What traditional areas can be modified so children rely less on paper-and-pencil tasks and instead use a makerspace mentality to explore similar concepts in more creative ways? Doing so will help them become innovators, graduating from school knowing how to solve a real-world problem in complex, collaborative, and creative ways. In an age when we cannot predict what jobs or technologies will exist when children are ready to enter the workforce, it's imperative to provide opportunities for them to engage in environments that promote twenty-first-century competencies. Makerspaces promote layered and multifaceted computational thinking as children become fluent speaking in "loose parts." They think analytically and creatively and express and communicate their ideas in various ways. Tinkering, experimenting, problem solving, and representing in a makerspace follow the same process as inquiry-based learning and computational thinking. Children identify patterns, break apart complex problems into smaller steps, organize and create a series of steps for arriving at a solution, and build a representation of data through simulations using their ideas in authentic ways. They communicate their ideas to others, and these in turn become incorporated into future explorations and designs. The makerspace provides the hardware that children use to be creators of their own knowledge. The possibilities are as limitless as the children's imaginations.

## Cultivating a Makerspace and Growth Mindset Using Read-Alouds

Read-alouds are an excellent way to inspire children to think of themselves as creators and innovators, using the simple everyday objects they have regular access to. By exploring resilient characters in high-quality books, children will be introduced to the maker process and mindset.

## Using Books to Inspire Making

**Materials:** high-quality books that incorporate making and a maker's mindset, including *Not a Box* (Antoinette Portis), *Not a Stick* (Antoinette Portis), *The Most Magnificent Thing* (Ashley Spires), *Rosie Revere, Engineer* (Andrea Beaty), *Beautiful Oops!* (Barney Saltzberg), *What Do You Do with an Idea?* (Kobi Yamada)

**Instructions:** Spend time exploring each book together with the children. As you read, point out the illustrations and what is happening in each part of the story. Help the children explicitly notice and name each part of the story to understand it more deeply. Engage them in rich questioning throughout the text to uncover their ideas about the character's process and make rich text-to-self, text-to-text, or text-to-world connections. At the beginning of your maker journey, use the book as a mentor text and place it along with loose parts in a designated center to encourage children to explore the process of making from the story.

**Observations:** What do the children notice in the words and illustrations of each story? Can they connect to the characters and share their own experiences of persevering in activities at school and beyond? Do they make connections between books and identify characteristics of a growth mindset? What ideas emerged from the story for further exploration in the classroom? Are children inspired to try something new or make something interesting after reading?

**Next Steps:** Place books in prominent areas around the classroom for easy retell access and as visual reminders for the children. Create an anchor chart with the children that summarizes characteristics of a growth mindset that can be displayed in the classroom. Encourage them to reflect on their lives and write personal stories of when they faced difficult situations and persisted until they experienced success. Share these stories with one another and a partner class to encourage continued emphasis on growth mindset. ■

Helping children see that loose parts can fit together to create a bigger design is key for computational thinking. Starting slowly with the design process for identifying and solving the problem—asking questions, imagining solutions, planning a project to explore ideas further, creating a prototype, testing and refining it, and sharing it with others—encourages children to become comfortable with the process and take risks in their explorations. Small, easy projects build children's confidence as they complete projects of interest at their own rates. Children who practice making in small, increasingly difficult projects will feel positively about their work and be inspired to try more challenging designs. The following activities will help children see how small pieces can fit together and form bigger parts of a more complex creation while building their mindset and interest in making in the classroom.

## Chalkboard Roads and Chalk Block Structures

**Materials:** variety of different sizes of wooden blocks, chalkboard paint, chalk, erasers, mini cars and trucks

**Instructions:** Paint the wooden blocks with the chalkboard paint and let dry. Some pieces may require a second coat of paint. Encourage the children to draw on the pieces and turn them into various parts of a play scene, such as roads and buildings for a community. They can brainstorm their design, draw on the pieces and fit them together, and use other loose parts (such as cars, mini animals, and little people) to creatively role-play. Piecing the blocks together helps the children see how smaller components come together to form a more complete project. The roads and buildings can be moved in different ways yet still fulfill the same goal (for example, the wooden pieces forming a road can be arranged in a variety of ways yet still allow cars to travel back and forth).

Blocks covered with chalkboard paint are open-ended building materials that can be easily manipulated by children.

**Observations:** Are the children able to piece together the smaller parts into a more complex creation? Do they notice that the pieces form a larger map or pathway? Can they build on previous designs to make more complex creations with practice? Are the children able to incorporate other materials from the classroom to enhance their play?

**Next Steps:** Offer these materials in the construction center and encourage continued use. Ask the children if there are other materials that they feel could enhance their work. Encourage them to draw blueprint-like representations of their community creations on paper. Take photos of the children's creations and encourage them to add written descriptions that can be incorporated into a community building book for future reference. ■

Making can also be an easy provocation for exploration at the art center, using very few materials that are simple to gather and assemble—recycled loose parts, paper, glue, and cardboard. The complex math and language skills and expectations contained in these rich experiences invigorated our program and surpassed past lessons that I had used to fulfill similar standards. Being open to looking at math and language through a maker's lens was key for this pedagogical shift in my thinking.

## Paper Sculpting

**Materials:** strong and shallow cardboard base with edges, various lengths and colors of construction-paper strips, large pompoms, strong adhesive such as tape or glue

**Instructions:** Encourage the children to manipulate the paper in different ways by folding, twisting, and tearing it, creating zigzags, loops, and curves. Demonstrate to the children that they can secure both ends of the paper to the cardboard base, creating interesting paper sculptures, such as zigzag lines, curves, and tunnels. Once they have assembled their paper lines into a complex and layered sculpture, add a pompom or small marble to the box and encourage them to slowly and gently roll it from side to side. This will move the pompom around the sculpture, under the paper twists, and through the curves. The children will recognize that their design helps or hinders the movement of the pompom, and the harder and faster they manipulate the box, the more frantic the pompom's movements become. Encourage the children to experiment with new designs, creating even more complex paths for the pompom to travel, perhaps establishing a starting and ending position and awarding points in their game.

A maze is created by gluing the ends of paper strips to the inside of a box. A marble can be rolled around and underneath the strips.

**Observations:** Can the children easily manipulate the materials? Do they work independently or collaboratively on their projects? Do the children persist when the materials do not stay in place or work the way they envisioned? Do the children experiment with one another's creations? Can the children add additional materials to create a dramatic context for their work (such as adding a picture of a hamster and turning the structure into a hamster playground)?

**Next Steps:** Encourage the children to share their designs and creations in a community sharing circle to receive feedback from their peers so that designs can be improved and children can learn from one another's experiences and mistakes. ■

## Cardboard Pinball Games

**Materials:** strong and shallow cardboard base with edges, variety of loose parts (caps, buttons, tubes), strong adhesive such as glue or tape, marbles

**Instructions:** Demonstrate for the children how the loose parts can be semipermanently affixed to the bottom of the cardboard box using tape. This first step is important because the use of tape instead of glue allows the children to modify their designs before permanently sticking objects to the cardboard. Children can tinker with the designs of their games and place loose parts in different ways to create mazes or pinball-style games through which they will move their marbles. The marbles travel through tubes, around obstacles, and along certain paths, and are propelled around the games as children gently roll their cardboard boxes from side to side with their hands. The children can establish starting and ending points and award points for moving the marbles around and through certain obstacles in their games. Once the children are satisfied with their designs, permanently secure the game parts to the cardboard bases with strong glue.

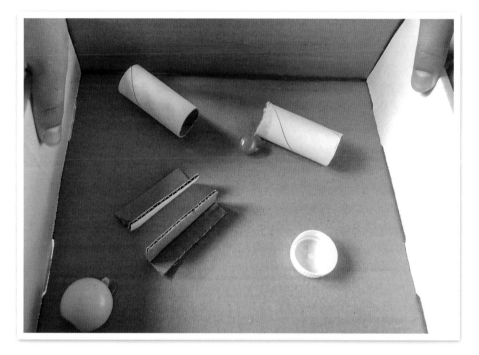

A cardboard pinball-style game is made using recycled parts affixed to a cardboard box.

**Observations:** How do the children repurpose materials? What strategies do they use when experiencing a problem in their designs? Do they persist with the task and build on previous designs or move quickly in their work? Are the children able to provide constructive feedback to their peers when considering their designs? What other materials might be added to enhance the experience?

**Next Steps:** Consider enlisting the help of older-grade coding buddies or adult volunteers to scaffold this experience and provide guided support for children. Display finished designs in the classroom, and the children can use one another's games during free-choice time. Encourage the children to share feedback and suggestions for improvement after playing another child's game. Incorporate feedback into future designs, or revise the games into newer versions. ■

In addition to creating games, rethinking how we might evolve some of our favorite math tools, like geoboards, created numerous possibilities for making that also embedded many rich and complex math ideas into collaborative building.

## Pegboard Construction

**Materials:** large pieces of wooden pegboard, golf tees, wooden dowels, nuts and bolts, elastics, marbles

**Instructions:** Display the piece of horizontal pegboard in an open area where children have access to all sides, such as on a table. The children can manipulate the pegboard in a variety of ways. Golf tees or nuts and bolts can be secured in the different holes, creating interesting patterns and designs. When elastics are stretched and secured on these, the pegboard becomes a giant geoboard, and the children can explore geometric and spatial-reasoning skills by manipulating them in different ways. Once the children are comfortable creating with the pegboard, encourage them to create mazes using the elastics as gutters to move the marble around the board without it falling off. The pegboard will be transformed into a giant marble run, and the children can create obstacles and other interesting paths through which the marble can travel. The pegboard's evolution from large geoboard to complex marble run will encourage children to engage in the design process as they incorporate previous knowledge and experience and use the problem-solving process to arrive at a final creation.

Wooden dowels are placed in pegboard holes to create an easy geoboard. Shapes can be formed by stretching elastics over the dowels.

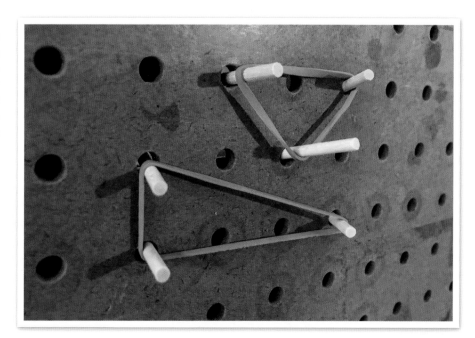

**Observations:** This activity requires control over fine-motor muscles in hands and fingers. Are the children able to successfully manipulate the materials? Do they persist when faced with a challenge in their design? Do the children incorporate knowledge from other areas (such as geometry) into their work? What other materials might be added to improve the experience and enhance the design process for the children?

**Next Steps:** Continue to offer this as an activity for children during free-choice time. Encourage them to incorporate additional materials from the classroom to create more complex designs and runs. Mount the pegboards in different ways (vertically on the wall, flat on a table) to change the children's perspectives and challenge their thinking. ∎

Sensory bins are an essential component of early primary classrooms for many reasons (Dietze and Kashin 2018). Young children learn best when they can explore interesting materials using their senses—seeing, smelling, touching, and hearing. Sensory play provides opportunities for children to collaborate and explore authentic math concepts by manipulating the tools and materials in different ways, often incorporating many aspects of computational thinking as they experiment and problem solve creating complex runs. Creating runs helps children explore cause-and-effect relationships in a variety of ways. They use problem-solving to create and refine new and exciting ways of moving sensory materials. Sensory activities can also be very calming and soothing as children slowly and carefully observe the textures of the materials, letting them trail through their fingers as they work and play!

## Complex Sensory Runs

**Materials:** flexible tubes of various lengths, different sizes of funnels, measuring cups and spoons, bowls, large sensory bin, various sensory materials (water, sand, kernels, beads, marbles)

**Instructions:** Fill your sensory bin (or large container) with one kind of material. Place the tools (tubes, funnels, cups, and so forth) in a basket next to the bin. Encourage the children to experiment with measuring and moving the materials in different ways (for example, pouring water from a cup or through a tube). As the children become more familiar with the tools, they can combine them in different ways (like attaching a funnel to the end of a tube). Add layers to heighten the play and encourage more opportunities for cause and effect to be explored (such as adding boxes to the tops or sides of the table with holes cut out for tubes and other materials to be woven throughout).

A variety of sensory materials are provided for children to use in open-ended explorations with sand and water.

**Observations:** Are the children able to see the relationship between recycled pieces and plan complex uses for transporting sensory materials in different ways? Are they able to use their understanding of the properties of materials and chose suitable tools (for example, kernels may not fit through small tubing)? Do they use mathematical terminology in context? Are they able to incorporate previous experiences with measurement and other conservation activities into their play? What ideas for more complex building do they have?

**Next Steps:** Encourage the children to create more complex designs after studying books and other sources of real-world information (sewer plans, pipes in the building, and so on). Community and parent experts (plumbers, engineers) can volunteer to work with children at this center. Children can design their runs on paper first and then be challenged to build what they've envisioned. Laminate and display photos of completed projects near the sensory areas as inspiration for future design work. ■

Once the children understand that they can create situations in which materials are purposely moved in a variety of complex ways, they can use their imaginations to create Rube Goldberg machines. Searching for "Rube Goldberg machines" online will result in hundreds of videos showcasing different inventions that can inspire your learners to tinker and create their own cause-and-effect system using loose parts.

## Rube Goldberg Machines

**Materials:** large working area, variety of loose parts, adhesive materials including tape and glue

**Instructions:** Spend time discussing what a Rube Goldberg machine is. Showing the children a variety of videos may enrich their building schema and inspire them to think creatively in the classroom. It's perfectly okay if you notice them copying some of the designs from the videos to understand the chain-reaction process more closely. Once the children are comfortable, challenge them to reflect on an everyday event or activity that they'd like to explore in their own design process (like flipping a switch or powering a car down a ramp). Using loose parts that can move (marble on a track, toy car), encourage them to create mini Rube Goldberg machines. Start small—one or two chain reactions at first—and then slowly build on a design that works. Once the children have created something, capture the machine in action by videotaping the process from start to finish and sharing the video beyond the classroom using social media (#maker, #makerspace, #RubeGoldberg).

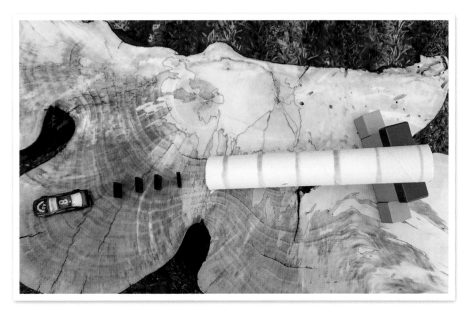

A simple Rube Goldberg machine is created using loose parts. A marble dropped through the tube will knock down the dominoes and cause the car to roll forward.

**Observations:** Are the children able to plan out designs incorporating simple cause-and-effect reactions? Do they plan out their designs ahead of time, or are they creating as they go? Do they persist when problems occur in their designs, or do they quickly change course to something else? Are the children able to work collaboratively on a single design, or do they spend time on independent projects?

**Next Steps:** Encourage the children to create a complex Rube Goldberg machine over a long period of time, leaving the creation out permanently in a designated classroom spot that children can return to over time. Children can plan their machine at first using drawn blueprints and gather required materials from the classroom (and their homes if donations are necessary). The more complex the creation gets, the more of a challenge it might be to persist when problems or disagreements in design occur. Support the children by reminding them to follow their plan and stay true to the intention of their design. ■

## Everyday Inventions

**Materials:** variety of loose parts, adhesive materials, including tape and glue, paper, writing materials

**Instructions:** Engage the children in a whole-group conversation to consider and discuss a problem that might exist in the classroom (for example, the door won't stay propped open). Ask them for help designing and creating an invention to help solve this problem. The children can sketch plans for their invention on paper before gathering loose parts and adhesive materials. Once they are comfortable with their design, they can begin tinkering with materials and testing their inventions to see if they can in fact help solve the problem. As the children work through the design process, they can revise their plans as needed. Once a child has invented a successful creation, take photos of the new device and add them to the class invention book. The children can name their invention and write an accompanying paragraph to describe the process they followed.

**Observations:** Are the children able to critically consider the classroom environment and brainstorm areas for improvement? Can they transfer their ideas to a paper design and use it to successfully follow the creation process? How do they respond when faced with a challenge in their work or if their design fails to achieve what they hoped it would? Do they persevere in completing the project?

**Next Steps:** Have the children review the school to see if there is a bigger project to explore. Share community problems with your class and invite the children to think about ways they can help solve bigger problems in their immediate world. Inviting community members to assist children with projects in the classroom is a great way to reach out beyond the walls of the school. Children can share their inventions with the greater community by blogging or tweeting about them, using the school account. ■

## Plastic-Brick Marble Runs

**Materials:** large collection of plastic bricks such as Legos, flat click-in base, marbles, paper, writing materials

**Instructions:** Show the children online pictures of intricate outdoor labyrinths if you feel they require encouragement and inspiration before beginning this task. The photos can often be an interesting conversation starter, as many children may have never had an opportunity to build these before. First ask children to draw blueprints for their mazes on pieces of paper of equal size to their mats. Once the children are satisfied with their designs, encourage them each to place bricks in pathways on a horizontal base to create a complex labyrinth through which a marble needs to travel. The marble can be placed at the starting position in the maze and moved when a child gently rolls the base from side to side. The more complex the pathway, the more challenging it will be to maneuver the marble.

A child manipulates a marble through a maze he has constructed using plastic bricks.

**Observations:** Are the children interested in designing and constructing their own labyrinths? Do they have experience visiting or playing with these? Do they have a plan for how to design and construct one? How do the children problem solve when running into difficulties with their designs?

**Next Steps:** If the children express continued interest in labyrinths, encourage them to create more complex mazes that they can walk through in the outside play yard. Use different materials, such as recycled boxes and large wooden blocks. They can continue to search online for large outdoor labyrinths to see the many interesting ones constructed throughout the world. ■

Continue encouraging children to consider how they might design and create innovative versions of everyday objects that can be used for a specific purpose. In our classroom, children spent time each morning looking through our windows and watching the bustle on the busy road in front of our school. They became fascinated with the different vehicles they observed, studying them in depth so they could better understand their design and function (garbage trucks had a large, powerful fork that could easily lift the filled bins placed by the road; police cars had sirens and lights to help warn others to get out of the way when they were racing to an emergency). I incorporated the children's interest in vehicle function and design so they could create their own interesting cars to be used in a class race down the large hill in our play yard.

## Vehicle Races

**Materials:** information sources about vehicles (books, websites, community experts), variety of large and small loose parts, adhesive materials, stopwatch or timer, paper, writing materials including pencils and crayons

**Instructions:** After exploring vehicles in depth, encourage the children each to design their own car or truck by first drawing a picture on paper. Encourage them to consider what they know about vehicles and incorporate this into their design. (Do they want their car to be fast? Stable? Able to carry a heavy load?) Once the children have a plan, provide adequate time and resources for them to build their design using loose parts. If this is too challenging for younger children, enlist the help of older coding buddies or ask parents to assist by volunteering time in the classroom.

The children can test their designs by using them on the track (rolling them down the large ramp or hill to be used in the race) or implementing the predetermined criteria to be used at the end of the competition (such as carrying the heaviest load). Once all the children have designed and created their vehicles, challenge them to compete. If you are observing whose car is the fastest when rolling down a ramp or hill, take time to let each child test their design and use the timer to track results. Invite them to observe their vehicle in action, make notes for how to improve its performance, and spend time revising their design to

*Simple vehicles can be made from wooden craft pieces.*

improve its output. This challenge doesn't have to happen in one day—organize it as a center where the children can work for longer periods of time. They can also design and build complex obstacles to use when testing their creations.

**Observations:** Are the children able to follow the design sequence successfully from start to finish? Are they interested in the challenge? Do they use mistakes in their design as opportunities for learning? Do they consider and implement their peers' suggestions for improvement into the design? Are they engaged in the experience? Do they persevere when the design doesn't perform as expected? What are their ideas for enhancing the experience or creating new challenges to follow?

**Next Steps:** Consider sharing your challenge on social media and inviting virtual pen pals and other invested followers also to design, test, refine, and share their creations with a larger global audience. Examine designs created outside the classroom and replicate them for experimentation into your work. Discuss what is successful in other designs, and consider implementing similar characteristics into your creations. Take photos of the creations so that the children can write about them and add information to an inventor's handbook to be kept in the building area of the classroom. ■

Makerspaces can be magical places that encourage children to engage in rich creation and problem-solving. When children are motivated to explore self-directed areas of interest, opportunities are plentiful to engage them in computational thinking that emphasizes creativity, collaboration, innovation, and perseverance. Experience tinkering with loose parts will help children develop skills and knowledge that will benefit them in future coding activities.

# CHAPTER 5

# Creating a Sense of Community Using Unplugged Coding

*The children were busy at work, carefully sculpting farm animals and placing them among paper bales of hay and modeling-clay trees.*

*"I'm putting my cows here, next to the grassy field, because that's where I remember the farmer feeding them."*

*"No, I think the cows were beside the red barn, not the row of trees. Put them over toward me a little bit more. I'm going to make a henhouse and put the chicks inside it. Cows and chicks live in different houses."*

*"I'll create the tractor path on the outside—I'm going to use pebbles and push those into brown modeling clay to look like real rocks in the dirt."*

*We had recently explored a local farm after the children had engaged in a rich inquiry researching animals. On the field trip, they had documented interesting things they noticed by taking photos using the class tablet. Upon returning to the classroom, they hoped to re-create as much of the farm as they could, sculpting animals from clay and creating the structures and landmarks they observed, using loose parts and other materials. Once the farm was built, they planned to retell their journey through it, mapping out the field trip from start to finish in a variety of ways.*

Children are innately curious. From the early moments of infancy to the first time they walk through our school door, they are striving to better understand their world by using all their senses. Learning through direct experience is essential for children to be successful in integrated, inquiry-based classrooms. Experiential learning occurs when children reflect deeply on the final results or solutions they have generated in their complex problem-posing endeavors (Dietze and Kashin 2018). To transform experience into new knowledge, the process needs to be meaningful to children in some way. Experiential learning is always "spiraling" as children continue to investigate the world around them, incorporating previous experiences into new explorations and knowledge creation rather than following a fixed, linear path. This cycle continues over and over as children build on previous knowledge and experiences and integrate new observations and connections over time. Their schemas grow and evolve with each new inquiry, becoming deeper and more complex.

In Reggio Emilia, the school is not the only place for learning (Wein 2008, 2014). As seen in the vignette above, children are taken out for day trips and have the opportunity to explore and gain real-life experiences within their local community and beyond. The outdoors offers children numerous opportunities to make connections to their own lives and learn by physically manipulating their environments and appreciating all that nature has to offer through their senses. Children exploring the world beyond the school will realize their fundamental connections to each other and to the world around them through many relationships. In the vignette, it's evident that the children were working to create a deeper understanding of the intricacies of the farm by re-creating their experiences after visiting it (discussing where the animals lived, what the farmer fed them, and the vehicles used on the farm). Although it may not be obvious at first, they are coding their experiences on the farm, engaging in metacognition by deconstructing and interpreting their own thinking through the process of artistic making. Outdoor experiences that might inspire deeper inquiry and understanding include the following:

> looking at areas of the school less traveled by the children, including "behind the scenes" rooms, main offices, and hallways used by staff and older students

> exploring the schoolyard in depth, including grassy areas or treed perimeters

> walking to nearby trails, streams, fields, or wooded lots

> visiting local parks and nature sanctuaries within walking distance

> taking regular community walks around the local neighborhood and studying community buildings and landmarks in depth

> observing bustling city streets, stores, parks, subway systems, and rails

> considering what may be hidden deep underground or up high in the sky

## Connecting the Local Community to Reggio Emilia

Reggio Emilia–inspired educators cultivate and support a safe and nurturing classroom environment where children and their families see themselves reflected in the learning space and work together toward collective learning and understanding (Wein 2008, 2014; Wurm 2005). Families offer support to schools and help shape policy by attending events and sharing their experiences and input regarding their children's lives in multiple ways. The presence of children is felt throughout the town as their learning is visible everywhere, displayed throughout parks and in shop windows, homes, and even the local theater. This honors children as democratic members of the community who contribute to the local culture in a variety of ways.

Schools are the heart of a community. In Reggio Emilia, education is considered the focal point of society, and families are welcomed to provide the best experience possible for all children (Wein 2014; Wurm 2005). Bringing learning directly into the community helps forge this connection. Working beyond the classroom space can empower children's thinking, invite partners inside the school, and encourage the community to more closely examine and appreciate the rich work of young children. It makes sense, then, that using all the local community has to offer will support children's personal and collective explorations and inspire rich inquiry that can lead to in-depth computational-thinking activities.

In our classroom, we have found that using the local community as inspiration for unplugged coding activities has had many benefits:

> helping children recognize their important place in our big world

> encouraging children's perceptions of the impact they can have on their local community

> illustrating for children how local environments ultimately connect together to form a greater place

> building a sense of belonging, pride in community, and patriotism in children

> using positional language in meaningful ways as children explore location and proximity

> giving rich context to children's unplugged games and activities

> building skills for children who are interested in coding but need more structure and support

> connecting children's interest in maps, ramps, and pathways to computational thinking

Although the two may seem unrelated at first, helping children explore their local community using various strategies and tools, including observation and mapmaking, link learning directly to unplugged coding activities. When one uses a coding board, or another method of communication that uses a set of instructions or an algorithm within the parameter of a story, it helps take the user on a path from start to finish, incorporating a setting, characters, and story line. The coding becomes a shareable project that can take other users far beyond the realm of the school directly into the experience. Community exploration helps children understand how the world around them is constructed (people, places, and things), and with this exploration, they can move from physical representation of place and time to more abstract digital representations. Exploring one informs the other.

Marina Umaschi Bers (2018) reminds us that coding activities that encourage children to consider and incorporate the greater community also provide a mechanism for "giving back to others" and making the world a more positive, productive place to be. Sharing children's work beyond the walls of the classroom encourages community support and participation within education, as stakeholders such as families, friends, and neighbors can recognize and celebrate the achievements of young children. When the work involves the community, there are multiple entry points for observers to use to connect with the work and consider the implications it might have in their lives and beyond. Children can reach out to children in other areas of the world, using the internet and social media, sharing information about their community through coding projects and learning about new and interesting places through the coding work of others. Exploring the community can lead children on many interesting journeys. I have always thought of children who code as travelers and of coding paths as our maps. They have a start and end position and help a child move an object or character in a specific sequence from beginning to end.

In previous chapters, I shared some of the basics of inviting children to explore unplugged coding concepts using a grid. But what about children who are not yet ready for the grid? In our classroom, I have used many simple yet effective tools and games to help children recognize the purpose of a coding path, taken out of the intricacies of the coding grid. These easy to implement and practice activities prepare children for later coding work and also serve as a segue to more complex community coding activities. If unplugged coding on a board is a journey, the following activities are short day trips children can take to build their coding confidence and abilities one activity at a time.

## Creating Coding Paths with Foam Mats

**Materials:** multiple sets of interlocking foam mats

**Instructions:** Demonstrate to the children how the pieces can puzzle together in different ways. Rather than asking children to assemble the mats in a traditional square or rectangle shape, show how the pieces can be arranged one at a time and from side to side to form a long and jagged pathway. Choose one end to be the starting position and stand on it. Ask the children to watch how you can slowly step from mat to mat until you reach the end of the path. As

Foam mats are connected together in a path for children to follow.

you move, articulate the number and direction you are moving ("I'm moving forward one, to the right one, forward two more places, now left one"). Take the mats apart and encourage the children to help you rearrange them into a new pathway. Add more mats to increase the complexity and challenge of maneuvering through the path. Repeat the process of moving through the path by stepping on each piece and articulating your movements aloud. Encourage the children to consider the number of mats used and where they are placed. When the children are ready, add a written component to the experience by placing arrow cards down next to the path to describe the sequence users follow when moving from start to finish. Encourage the children to read the algorithm together with you as a volunteer moves through the pathway. Take turns creating and following pathways until the children appear comfortable and are ready to explore the materials independently.

**Observations:** Do the children understand how the pieces fit together? Do they default to puzzling the pieces together so that no spaces are left in between (like a puzzle), or do they understand that the pieces can move in multiple directions? Are they able to follow the paths with their bodies? Do they give story lines to their paths? Can they orally articulate the coding path used before putting it into action?

**Next Steps:** When the children are ready, consider adding arrow coding cards to indicate direction. Bring foam mats to other areas of the school, such as the gym or outdoors, so the children can incorporate them into their own games and explorations. ■

## Straw-and-Connector Paths

**Materials:** very large collection of straws and connectors

**Instructions:** Demonstrate to the children how the straws and connectors can be assembled into squares that can be linked together to form complex paths. To challenge the children, create paths that have variety to them, requiring a user to move left and right, forward and backward many times. Establish a starting and ending position, and model for the children how to move from square to square, articulating your movements as you go. Using a dry-erase board, record the coding sequence users must follow when moving along the path. Encourage the children to rearrange the straws and connectors into new positions. Issue challenges to the children when designing and building their coding sequences ("Can you build a path that travels all the way across our classroom?" "Can your path go around two tables?").

Straws and connectors are arranged into a path for children to follow by stepping or jumping in each square.

**Observations:** Are the children able to physically manipulate the straws and connectors? Do they work together to create a large, collaborative creation, or in isolation? Are the children able to picture the entire project and plan their work, or do they experiment and create as they go?

**Next Steps:** Challenge the children to turn their two-dimensional squares into cubes and link these together in different three-dimensional paths. Can they see the path this new sequence creates? Can they move an object (like a toy plane or stuffed animal) through the path and orally describe each movement? What other ideas do they have for what these three-dimensional pieces can be used for? ■

## Coding with Magnets

**Materials:** large collection of magnetic square building tiles, arrow coding cards

**Instructions:** Use a vertical metallic surface to provide a different perspective for children observing this activity. Model how the tiles can be placed next to each other to create a mini vertical coding path. Determine the starting and ending positions of the path. Point your finger at the starting position, and as you articulate the coding sequence, move your finger so that it follows the direction of the path. Create a new pathway and ask the children to study the direction of movement from start to finish. Place the arrow coding card under each magnetic tile so that its direction is visible. Ask the children to articulate the sequence the path takes from start to finish.

A coding path is created from magnetic tiles. Arrow coding cards are used to indicate direction.

**Observations:** Do the children create simple or complex paths? Is there choice and variety in their paths so that users have a variety of ways to arrive at the final path? Do the children use correct positional language to describe direction and movement?

**Next Steps:** Ask the children for ideas that can enhance their paths. Can they add other magnetic loose parts to create obstacles or barriers that must be considered in their sequence? How can they use the paths in different ways? Provide different metallic bases for them to use (magnetic chalkboard, cookie tray) so they must work within the area of the surface, creating more complex and compacted paths to manipulate and maneuver. ∎

## Plastic-Brick Pathways

**Materials:** large collection of plastic bricks such as Legos, large click-in base or mat, variety of prewritten coding sequence cards

**Instructions:** Display the bricks in a basket next to the brick base. Offer the children their choice of one of the coding sequence cards. Place the card next to the brick base. Follow the directions outlined on the coding card by placing the first brick in the starting position on the base. Follow the directions, line by line, and place bricks on the base, building the full algorithm until you reach the end. Turn the card over to reveal the answer and see if your brick creation matches the coding path shown.

Children are challenged to create the path represented on the instruction card.

**Observations:** Are the children interested in creating the sequencing paths using the plastic bricks? Are their fine-motor skills strong enough to manipulate the small parts and intricacies in the design, or would larger bricks (such as Duplos) work better, depending on their developmental abilities? Do the children add loose parts to enhance their path and create their own story lines? Do they appear eager to design their own paths for others to follow?

**Next Steps:** Encourage the children to design, build, and record their own unique plastic brick paths for others to follow. Write them on instruction cards to be used by other children in their play. Consider using coding buddies to help scaffold and support the experience for children. ∎

## Creating Coding Paths with Pentominoes

**Materials:** large set of pentominoes, minifigures, paper, pencil

**Instructions:** Display the pentominoes in a large basket. On your working surface, piece together the pentominoes end to end to form a complex coding path (this is opposite of their intended use of being pieced together with no spaces in between). Pentominoes provide an extra challenge to children because of the complexities of their design and the way the five squares on each piece can fit together. This will create a complex path with multiple dead ends. Establish a story with characters (for example, the animals want to find each other). Code the directions from beginning to end, moving the character through the maze to reach the final point. Once you are satisfied with the movements the character took, record the code next to the path. Add more pieces or change the design to make it more complex. The children can design a background picture as a setting to support the story behind the sequence.

A pentomino path is created by placing pieces end to end.

**Observations:** Can the children manipulate the pentominoes into different paths? Are they able to articulate a successful sequence without ending up at a dead end? How much support and guidance do they require in this activity? Do they write their code in step-by-step instructions, or can they incorporate control structures such as loops into their design? Do they become easily frustrated when they encounter an error, or are they able to use the bug as an opportunity to refine their work?

**Next Steps:** Ask the children what other loose parts they feel would enhance their pentomino paths. Place these along with the collection of pentominoes in a large working area where the children can design, test, and refine complex paths over the course of many days. Encourage them to leave their works in progress and invite their friends to join in the creation of these collaborative projects. Print and laminate photos of the finished pentomino paths for the children to explore with dry-erase markers.                ■

## Exploring the Community through Coding

When children are comfortable working with tangible, constructed pathways, you can move on to additional coding activities. In our classroom, one of the first ways we used the local community to inspire our unplugged coding work was re-creating what we observed on school and community walks using pathways made of various materials. The pathways formed together to create systems by which the children could theoretically or realistically move objects from place to place. In a similar fashion to how we use roads and sidewalks to move from place to place, the various materials and loose parts children used in their STEM work (outlined in the following activities) became the physical foundation for understanding later coding systems. These algorithmic building blocks helped children use and understand abstract coding lines through the language of building. Before any work was completed in the classroom, we spent time reading in preparation for our walks, discussing how we could use technology (including the camera in our tablet) to capture pictures of our discoveries during neighborhood walks. As in other experiences, quality books read aloud and discussed with children can help build background knowledge and inspire conversation, leading to greater inquiry planning and implementation.

### Using Books to Explore Community

**Materials:** high-quality books about mapping and exploring the community, including *Mapping Penny's World* (Loreen Leedy), *Me on the Map* (Joan Sweeney), *Where Do I Live?* (Neil Chesanow), *Follow That Map!* (Scot Ritchie)

**Instructions:** Spend time exploring each book together with the children. As you read, point out the illustrations and what is happening in each part of the story. Highlight the different ways characters explored the world around them and recorded what they saw. Specifically highlight the maps included in the books and engage the children in a conversation about how they might use this knowledge in their own explorations in the community. If you are planning on taking the children to another part of the school, yard, or community, ask them for suggestions on how they might record what they see so that the information can be used in subsequent activities (such as taking photos on the tablet or recording observations by drawing pictures in a sketchbook). Engage the children in rich questioning throughout the text to uncover their ideas about the character's process and make rich text-to-self, text-to-text, or text-to-world connections. At the beginning of your community explorations, use the book as a mentor text and bring it with you for reference in your travels outside the classroom.

**Observations:** What do the children notice in each book? Are they able to use the illustrations to help support their understanding of location and direction? Do they make connections between the texts and their own lives and experiences? Do they extend the ideas presented in the books into their own play? Can the books be used as conversation prompts to help them plan for ways in which they might explore their immediate community and beyond?

**Next Steps:** Engage in a conversation with the children regarding the experiences in each book. Ask if they have an interest in exploring an unknown area of the school or their community. Plan with them how they might travel beyond their classroom. Seek the guidance of experts, gather materials, and invite partners to support and encourage. Reach out to the greater community to plan stops along the way, helping the children see new and interesting places and gathering information to be used in future coding activities. ∎

## Community Walks

**Materials:** tablets, cameras, writing tools, including pencils and markers, clipboards or journals, volunteers

**Instructions:** Once the children have considered the concept of community exploration through read-alouds, encourage them to venture out and explore beyond the classroom. Choose a place to visit, perhaps consulting the children as to where they'd like to go. You can make a list of places and have the children vote for their favorites, then spend time traveling to each one on subsequent community walks. Plan ahead for how children will collect and represent their observations while out of the classroom and collect what is needed before venturing out. Using a wagon to store needed items (tablets, clipboards, journals, writing materials) might make it easier to transport things on your walk, especially depending on the age of the children. Recruiting volunteers to accompany the children—older student buddies and family members—provides additional support to each child on the walk, helping them point out interesting features along the way and collecting observations to be used back in the classroom. Once back in the classroom, gather the children together on the carpet and ask them to share their observations and collected data from the walk. Use open-ended questions to prompt and guide the discussion.

**Observations:** What do the children notice on their walk? What interests or intrigues them? How do they interact with their surroundings and record their observations? Are they comfortable and familiar with their surroundings? What questions do they have during and after their walk?

**Next Steps:** Engage the children in a whole-group conversation after the walk. Ask them to share photos or drawings of their surroundings and discuss outstanding questions or concerns they might have. Challenge the children to incorporate their new experiences in some way. Perhaps they would like to explore a question or wondering further by doing a bit of research, or share information about their community in a new way (creating advertisements for a local building, writing a story about their experience, drawing a map). Ask the children how to share these new questions for exploration outside the classroom and with the greater community. ■

As children become comfortable and familiar with their neighborhood, they can begin to translate their observations to physical representations. Multiple visits will be needed to help children form a complete and familiar understanding about the world that exists beyond their school. Creating maps and other representations to tell the stories of children's travels is an effective way to integrate STEM and prepare children for subsequent unplugged coding explorations. In our classroom, children were always very eager to show their travels using different materials and representations (building a place using blocks and loose parts, creating dioramas of familiar settings, drawing large murals using butcher paper). Educators can encourage STEM thinking by asking questions while children work and providing support as they research and represent their understanding through various languages of creation (like drawing and building). These architectural plans will become the frameworks on which children draw in subsequent mapping and coding activities.

## Mapping the Community

**Materials:** drawing materials such as crayons, pencils, and markers, large sheet of mural or butcher paper, wooden blocks, recycled materials, including boxes and other loose parts (pegs, buttons, caps), tablet or computer

**Instructions:** Look through the children's diverse observations from their community walks (photos, drawings, writing). Choose a location to represent (schoolyard, neighborhood around the school). Place the butcher paper in a large working area and encourage the children to draw the footprint of their school in the middle. Using what they know about the sidewalk and road structure around the school, children can begin to draw the roadway grid in their community. Children can also refer to their independent travels in the neighborhood to help inform this project (like the path their school bus takes when traveling from home to school each day). Assist the children in this project by displaying an overhead Google Earth photo of the school and surrounding area so they can check the accuracy of their drawing. Once the children are satisfied that they have created an adequate representation, they can begin to fill in the map with recycled materials and loose parts representing buildings and other landmarks. Encourage them to add other details—trees, landscaping, vehicles, mailboxes—as they work over time. When the children have completed the map, question them to reinforce location and position as they describe points of reference to one another ("Where is your house on the map compared to our school?" "If you needed to mail a letter and were at school, where is the easiest

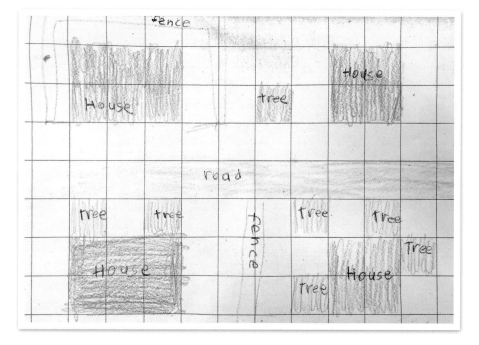

A child's bird's-eye drawing of his neighborhood.

place to find a mailbox?"). The children can then be challenged to create directions for moving along the map using the roads as a guide. Help the children use a bird's-eye view to describe movement on the map ("What directions would you give someone who wanted to travel from the school to the library?") and be as precise in their language as possible.

**Observations:** Are the children able to transfer their new knowledge to large collaborative representations? Can they each contribute a part to a larger creation, or do they work in isolation? Do they incorporate directionality into their designs? Do they see and understand how the small parts of the project fit together into a larger piece?

**Next Steps:** Place the large butcher paper map in a central location along with loose parts (figures, blocks, cars) and encourage the children to use it as a prop for acting out dramatic stories. They can retell their experiences traveling throughout the neighborhood (like walking from their house to school) or innovate adventures to role-play. As the children become comfortable using positional language and providing directions, encourage them to transfer these skills to another representation of location, mapping other familiar areas using grid paper. ∎

## Code the Classroom

**Materials:** large grid paper, writing materials, including pencils, crayons, and markers

**Instructions:** Encourage the children to consider a comfortable and familiar space, including the classroom. Model how a bird's-eye view can be used to examine one's immediate surroundings. Ask the children to look around the classroom and name the features and objects they see. Starting with permanent structures like windows and doors might be easiest. As the children name objects, draw their outline on the grid. If the children have a difficult time conceptualizing the map, choose a central feature to identify and draw first, like a communal carpet or teacher's desk. Slowly add the children's observations to the map—tables, chairs, shelves, and any other interesting feature of the room. Once they have helped create an adequate map of the classroom, encourage them to use unplugged coding language to maneuver the space. They can provide specific directions for moving from one place to the next using coding algorithms that include the direction and number of steps. They can also give just the directions from one spot to another and ask their friends to guess where they are moving on the map. Extend the activity by having the children draw blueprint maps of other interesting places, such as the playground or their bedrooms.

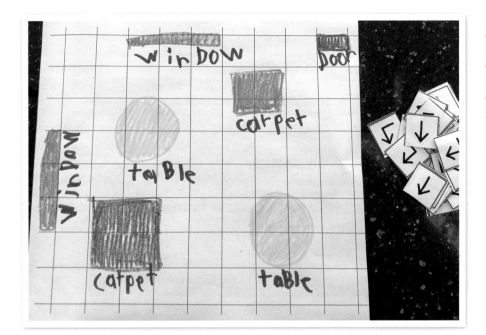

A child represents his classroom by drawing a map. He will use arrow coding cards to show the different paths he can walk in the space.

**Observations:** Can the children transfer what they see in their surroundings to a two-dimensional paper representation? Are their drawings to scale? Can they follow one another's maps?

**Next Steps:** Encourage the children to create grid maps of other areas of interest, perhaps places in the school or their homes. They can share and compare their maps with one another and give constructive feedback on how to improve their designs. As the children become more comfortable drawing and manipulating maps, encourage them to take their explorations further by incorporating them into their play. Children can create secret maps to lead one another on scavenger hunts around the classroom or play yard. ■

## Secret Maps

**Materials:** drawing materials such as markers, crayons, and pencils, grid paper

**Instructions:** Encourage the children to draw maps of their favorite places. They can use grid paper to create blueprints similar to the ones described in previous activities. Once the map is created, they can draw coding paths directly on the map using arrows, or they can provide coding algorithms and encourage their friends to follow the maps from start to finish. Encourage the children to incorporate the maps into their play (finding treasure on a hidden island, rescuing a lost puppy). Model the activity first by sharing a premade map. The children can use the coding algorithm to follow the steps on the map, traveling from place to place and ending up in a location where the teacher has previously hidden a secret message or prize.

**Observations:** Can the children successfully create and use maps in their play? Do they understand the concept of leading a user to a specific place? Do they challenge users by creating complex maps? What can they provide at the end of the map to entice users to want to explore further?

**Next Steps:** Ask the children how they can enhance their secret maps. Perhaps they can include a treasure or message to be found at the end of the secret map as an enticement for users. What other ideas do they have for enhancing the map play? ■

Children who incorporate grids into their coding experiences may be ready for describing locations using coordinates. A Cartesian plane (or coordinate plane) is a specialized grid with two perpendicular lines. The $x$ axis is horizontal and the $y$ axis is vertical. When using both of these axes together in a combination $(x, y)$, a user can describe any point of location on the grid using an ordered pair of letters or numbers. Although ordered pairs are not coding algorithms, they do lead users to a specific place on a two-dimensional plane. Children study the Cartesian plane extensively in subsequent math, so it's important that they build comfort and understanding early on through easy and entertaining games. Coordinate systems are also incorporated into coding work (like when characters in video games are moved around the screen using a coordinate system), so early exposure will help set the foundation for more complex coding later on in a child's life.

## Introducing the Coordinate Grid

**Materials:** coordinate grid, letter cards, number cards, blocks, dry-erase board, dry-erase marker

**Instructions:** Display the coordinate grid in the center of a large working space so that all children have a clear view. Place the letter cards along on the $x$ axis (horizontal line) and the number cards along the $y$ axis (vertical line). Explain to the children that each line has a specific name. When the $x$-axis and $y$-axis lines intersect, they form a coordinate. Demonstrate this by choosing a specific coordinate pair, articulating it aloud, and using your hands to run along the lines and motion to where they intersect. Place a block in that space on the grid and write the matching coordinate on the dry-erase board. Choose another block, articulate its coordinate aloud, and write it on the dry-erase board, then ask a volunteer to place the block on the grid in the correct location. Practice this

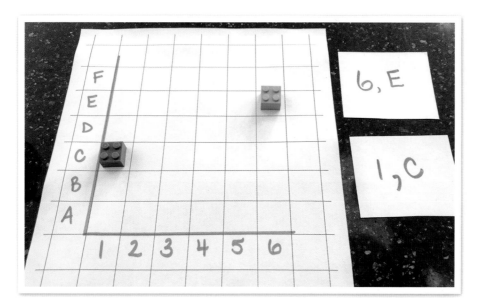

Letter cards indicate where blocks are to be placed on the grid.

as many times as needed to help the children understand how the grid works. Once they are comfortable, reverse the game. Ask a child to place a block on the grid without telling its coordinates and challenge volunteers to write the correct coordinates using the dry-erase board.

**Observations:** Do the children understand the concept of the grid? Can they see how the two points in the coordinates intersect to locate a specific place? Are they able to articulate their own coordinates and successfully lead another person to a specific place? Can they record their coordinates in a written format for someone else to follow? What other ideas for games do the children have in mind after playing this game?

**Next Steps:** Leave the grid and materials out in a center for the children to explore further. Encourage them to play games with one another, writing and finding different coordinates. They can incorporate other materials into their play and use the grid in different imaginative scenarios during the play block. ■

## Four-in-a-Row Coordinate Game

**Materials:** large Cartesian plane (draw this on chart paper with the *x* axis representing the numbers 1 to 6 and the *y* axis representing the letters A to F), two dice (one with the 1 one to 6 and another with the letters A to F), markers, blocks

**Instructions:** Display the grid to the children. Model how to roll both dice and use the results to form a coordinate. Once the coordinate is read, locate the spot on the grid and place a block on the square. The children can continue rolling the dice and filling in squares on the grid. Once they appear comfortable with the game, display a fresh, empty grid. Tell the children they are going to play "Four in a Row" using the coordinates. The game calls for two players or two teams to battle using the grid. Each player or team picks a color. Taking turns, they roll the dice, locate that coordinate on the grid, and place a block in it using their designated color. The first team to color four squares in a row on the grid wins.

*Two players take turns rolling and placing blocks on the grid until one player gets four in a row.*

**Observations:** Are the children able to successfully find and record their coordinates? Do they persevere in the activity when it takes a long time to get four in a row? Are they interested in the game? What other ways can they play?

**Next Steps:** If the children find it difficult to wait to get four in a row, consider modifying the experience and reducing the number of places needed in order to win. Encourage the children to think about different ways they can play the game. ■

## Race to Fill the Grid

**Materials:** small Cartesian plane (draw this on chart paper with the *x* axis representing the numbers 1 to 6 and the *y* axis representing the letters A to F), two dice (one with the numbers 1 to 6 and another with the letters A to F), large collection of loose parts (gems, blocks, shells), basket

**Instructions:** This game can be played by individual children or in a small group. Place the gems in a basket in the middle of a table. Each child continuously rolls the dice, identifying the coordinates and placing a gem in the corresponding place on the grid. Players roll and reroll, adding gems to their grids as fast as they can. The first player to fill their grid with gems in every spot wins! Vary the game by having the children place a gem in every square at the beginning of the game. As the coordinate dice are rolled, remove the gem located in that coordinate. The first player to empty their grid wins the game.

A child rolls the coordinate dice and fills her grid with blocks.

**Observations:** Are the children able to persevere through the activity even when it may appear to take them a long time to fill or empty their grid? Do they enjoy playing this game independently or in competition with a friend?

**Next Steps:** Consider differentiating the size of the grid to make it easier or more complex for users. Switch the loose parts placed on the grid to appeal to different children (such as small cars, gems, beads, or mini animals). ■

## Secret Coordinate Codes

**Materials:** large piece of grid paper with a drawn grid and random letters placed inside each coordinate

**Instructions:** Prior to playing the game with children, create a secret message or code and spell it out by placing the coordinates in order under the bottom of the grid. Encourage the children to look at each coordinate and locate where it is on the grid. Once the spot is found, identify the letter and write it under the coordinates. Repeat the process until each letter in the secret code is revealed and the children read the secret message.

*Children use the coordinates to find the letters to decode the secret message.*

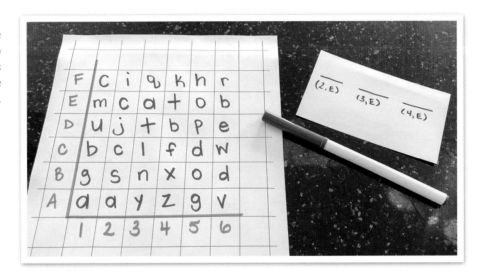

**Observations:** Are the children able to locate the correct place on the grid to retrieve the letters? Can they put the letters together into a word to read? Should the grid be modified in some way to make it easier or more challenging?

**Next Steps:** Encourage the children to create their own secret coordinate messages for one another. Copy, laminate, and place them in a writing area for the children to use over and over. Consider scrambling the letters the children find by using the coordinates so they must also decode the letters to uncover a message. This makes the game much more complex for children who are ready for the challenge. ■

Young children are fascinated by their place within the world around them. Adventures exploring their immediate surroundings, classrooms, schools, and neighborhoods provide rich context through which unplugged coding can be explored.

# CHAPTER 6

# Creative Coding

*The children were fascinated by a row of glass jars filled with different amounts of water colored with food coloring.*

*"I love this song—listen to Sam play it!" Julia said excitedly.*

*I watched as Sam gently tapped the jars in a rhythmic motion, playing a distinct melodic pattern.*

*"I wish we could keep this song! I want to share it with my mom!"*

*"I know . . . we can write the music just like singers do. We need to draw little circles on a paper. Then other people will be able to see the song and play it!"*

*The children gathered the materials and set to work. As Sam played a note by tapping a jar with his spoon, Julia recorded it by drawing a circle corresponding to the color of the water. By the time Sam was done performing his song, Julia had a line of different colored circles on her page, representing his composition.*

*"Now I can play Sam's song! I just have to follow the circles to know what to do!"*

Many educators know that playful exploration—including through the language of art—is essential for children's growth, health, and well-being, yet many of us still feel pulled in the direction of academic rigor and accountability, confined by standardized curriculum and assessment obligations. However, as educators we also recognize that the integration of twenty-first-century competencies into regular classroom experiences—collaboration, problem-solving, and creativity—are the elements that will most likely help prepare our children for life in an unknown future. How can educators honor and include the arts as authentic languages of learning while still fulfilling mandated expectations? In this chapter, I will share examples of how I have used joyful, creative ways to engage children in computational thinking and unplugged coding while invigorating their experiences with aesthetically playful games and activities.

## The Language of Art

Artistic exploration has always been considered an essential part of young children's lives, helping develop verbal and nonverbal expression, supporting cognitive and physical development, facilitating social and emotional abilities and connections, strengthening problem-solving skills, and promoting cultural awareness and sense of self (Isenberg and Jalongo 2018). Children can use diverse art forms, including visual art, drama, and music as languages of expression in unplugged coding activities. Art infuses children's memories and emotions into their work, enhancing symbolic communication and providing an avenue for self-expression when letters and numbers aren't sufficient representations of the depths of their experiences and emotions (Wexler 2004). Coding as an expressive experience encourages children to learn by doing—recognizing a process of exploration, identifying the various steps along the way, noticing and revising when problems arise, and sharing their thinking with a greater audience. Art nurtures and strengthens relationships in the educational environment as children and educators connect socially and emotionally to one another, supporting one another's interests and abilities using innovative tools and materials (Dietze and Kashin 2018). As an educator, I am most drawn to visual art in my classroom, and I have fond childhood memories of sculpting with clay and exploring color mixing with watercolors. Therefore I aspire to infuse the arts into coding activities whenever possible. I have observed some of the most quiet, reluctant children blossom through the artistic expressions they share within our classroom. I believe that the arts are one of the most powerful computational tools available to educators, the depths of the possibilities limited only by the imaginations of educators and children in the classroom.

In our Reggio Emilia–inspired program, children are encouraged to use their wonder and curiosity about the world as provocations for unplugged coding using hundreds of languages that explore and represent their emerging theories through numerous artistic forms and mediums. Finding a way to express oneself can often lead to self-discovery. Jinju Kang explains that "[the] means by which Reggio Emilia schools encouraged children to build their languages . . . increased the possibility of children developing and representing their own ideas, feelings, and thoughts" (2007, 47). When children learn the art of self-expression, they become free to communicate with others and exchange ideas in limitless ways, leading to complex collaboration and social interaction. Computational thinking is evident as children experiment, problem solve, and communicate their ideas using symbolic language. Educators can also use artistic inspiration for many of the more organized whole- and small-group coding games and activities that are presented in this chapter.

Educators can help shape children's artistic explorations in computational thinking through many considerations in the classroom:

> creating a safe and supportive environment

> emphasizing the process of making as more important than the final product

> providing a wealth of open-ended materials

> understanding that the arts are symbolic language for children and often the precursor to subsequent more structured representations of language, including reading and writing

> encouraging children to share the stories behind their creations through thoughtful questioning and conversation

> encouraging the use of art as a legitimate method of exploration and communication

> including children's artistic representations in the documentation displayed around the learning environment

> sharing children's artwork beyond the walls of the classroom and inviting community appreciation and conversation

Looking at the artistic explorations of Reggio Emilia encourages us to consider what role art might play in the computational thinking of the young children in our care. How might we harness the inspiration of the arts and use them to power unplugged coding, helping children emotionally connect to one another through aesthetic explorations and bringing joy and wonder to what can sometimes be regarded as a one-size-fits-all rote subject?

According to Umaschi Bers (2018), when children are immersed in an enjoyable, playful activity, they are often inspired to engage fully in the experience through intrinsic motivation. They persist through challenging problems and engage the support of their peers, often not wanting to end the activity even when it is time to clean up and move on to something different in the schedule. In the following activities, I hope to use the power of playful motivation to challenge children to use their love of music, creative movement, and role playing to engage them in unplugged coding. The following big-bodied movements engage children in enjoyable, social coding experiences that help them practice turn taking and negotiation in their interactions with one another. Adding music and props will enhance the experience and invite children to playfully code with their bodies.

## Creative Coding Dance

**Materials:** large paper, tape, various photos of dancing activities (spinning, clapping, finger snapping, foot stomping), markers, a device that plays music, QR codes that can be scanned for retrieving music online

**Instructions:** Gather the children in a large open area that provides ample room for them to engage in creative movement. Explain that they are going to help you code a dance sequence to follow. Start slowly. Ask the children to choose the order in which the dance actions should occur. Then place cards vertically in the correct sequence by sticking them with tape on the paper, creating a "dance algorithm" to follow. Demonstrate how to scan the QR code. Locate an upbeat musical selection online that the children will enjoy, and guide them through the dance code by pointing to each dance card in order and encouraging them to follow along by acting out the moves in their respective spaces. After a successful run-through, ask the children to challenge themselves by creating a more complex code. Continue to add more dance cards to the sequence and determine approximately how many counts/beats they will spend on each card before moving on to the next.

Once they appear comfortable, introduce a control structure like looping to create a more complex code for the children to follow. Just as before, start slowly. Place the dance cards in vertical order, but this time indicate how repeats will happen for each action by preceding the card with a number. For example, if the number 5 is placed before the "clap" card, this means that children need to clap five times when the card is reached in the sequence (clap, clap, clap, clap, clap). Play music and invite the children to once again follow the code and dance together. When they appear ready, differentiate the activity again by creating a more complex loop to follow. Instead of looping the same action over and over, group specific actions together and then circle these along with a number to indicate how many times a loop should occur. For example, the actions "clap," "stomp," "twirl" can be grouped and looped so that each time this sequence occurs, it must be repeated in that order for the specific number of times indicated in the code. A 6 (clap, stomp, twirl) means that children are following this pattern six times when the loop occurs.

**Observations:** Pay attention to whether the children are able to follow the sequence outlined in the dance algorithm. Are they able to follow along with limited prompting from a teacher? Can they easily implement the loops without assistance? How comfortable do they appear in the activities? What other actions or props can be included to enhance the experience and invite continued participation from children?

Looped coding cards indicate the order in which dance moves are to be performed.

**Next Steps:** Place all required materials (dance cards, blank cards that children can use to draw additional dance moves, a tablet, musical QR codes) in a classroom center or basket to be brought outdoors so children can continue creating and enacting their own unique dance routines. Consider what additional props might be added to enhance the play (colorful scarves, musical instruments), encouraging greater variety and complexity of movement and creating more involved dance coding. ■

## Roll and Move Coding Dice

**Materials:** three large foam coding dice

**Instructions:** Transform three large foam dice into "coding dice" by taping six photos of animals on one, directions on another (forward, backward, left, right, up, down), and the numbers 1 to 6 on the third. Gather the children in a large open area, such as the outdoor playground or a gym. The starting position should be in the middle of the area. Model for the children that when all three dice are rolled, the results can display a fun way of "coding" physical actions, resulting in creative and silly movement. For example, if these three dice were rolled—the number 6, a bear, and forward—children would have to move forward six paces while acting like a bear. The "up" and "down" directions are open to interpretation, so the children can be consulted on what that might look like in your space, or you can substitute other directions that might be easier for your children to conceptualize. Remind them that the movements are from their positional perspective, so they are the ones moving their bodies according to the dice.

*A variety of dice can be used in creative movement games.*

**Observations:** Do the children seem to understand that the dice represent three different concepts—movement, location, and role play? Are they able to coordinate their actions and move collectively? Are the directions too complicated, and would differentiating them increase student success and comfort in the activities? Can the dice be modified to incorporate current student interests and engage children more deeply in the activity?

**Next Steps:** Challenge the children to swap out the animals, directions, and numbers for more complicated movements. These can relate to current interests and inquiries. Consider placing the dice in a basket and offering them as an option during activities time (perhaps in a corner of the room with a large carpet) or incorporating them during outdoor centers and gym time by offering them as an optional center. ■

## Creative Movement Coding Race

**Materials:** three large foam coding dice, tape or chalk

**Instructions:** This game is best played in pairs. Transform three large foam dice into coding dice by taping six photos of animals on one, directions on another (forward, forward, forward, backward, backward, backward), and the numbers one to six on the third. Gather the children in a large open area, such as the outdoor playground or a gym. Create a horizontal line in the space (use masking tape on the ground or draw the line with chalk) for two children to stand on side by side. Create another long vertical line extending in front of and behind this line, forming four large quadrants. The children will move along this vertical line. Each child takes a turn rolling all three dice and moving their body in the code indicated. For example, if "3," "snake," and "forward" are rolled, the child will move forward in a snake-like fashion for three paces. Each child takes turns rolling the dice and moving forward or backward along the line. The first to reach the end of the vertical tape, regardless of whether it is in front of or behind them, wins the game.

**Observations:** How easily do the children understand the concept of moving according to the dice code? Are they pacing themselves in an equal manner so that each movement is a repetition of the previous one? Do they understand the concepts of forward and backward? Are they moving in a straight line?

**Next Steps:** Challenge the children to play with more players or in teams. Ask the children how else they would modify the game to make it more engaging or challenging. Incorporate their ideas into future versions.  ■

The arts evoke emotions as children use memories and connections to inspire new creation (Wexler 2004). Color, pattern, and tone help us better represent what we are thinking and feeling and communicate it more clearly to the outside world. Coding also requires clear and concise communication. The arts also draw us to the work of others, even when we were not a part of the creation process, and we become invested in better understanding their creations and points of view. Beautiful artwork invites us in, helping us join the artistic conversations of others and use our own experiences and ideas to enhance the conversation. Computational thinking can integrate the beauty of mathematics, making it an enjoyable, cross-curricular experience for children.

## Code a Song (Water and Spoon Melody)

**Materials:** clear glasses or jars, water, food coloring, crayons matching the food coloring, spoon, paper

**Instructions:** Fill each glass with different amounts of water. Add food coloring to make each glass a unique color. Show the children how to gently tap the glasses with the spoon to produce a different sound. Ask the children to hypothesize why the sounds are different from glass to glass. Encourage the children to volunteer to play a song by tapping the glasses in different orders. Encourage the children to attempt to reproduce familiar melodies (such as "Twinkle, Twinkle Little Star") or create patterns using the sounds. Once the children are comfortable using the spoon and glasses as musical instruments, demonstrate how to record the music in a code by drawing colorful circles in the order the glasses are to be played. Model recording a child's song as they play it for the group, then encourage the children to take turns playing a recorded song by following the color algorithm, or experiment with creating their own.

A song is coded by recording the order in which the glasses are to be tapped with the spoon.

**Observations:** How comfortable do the children appear playing their songs? Is there variety in the rhythm and melody of their musical exploration? Do they appear to understand the purpose of recording the songs using circles on paper? How else might the children want to represent their notation? Do they have other ideas for how to use the materials? Can they follow the musical codes of their peers?

**Next Steps:** Provide empty jars, a container of water, food coloring, and writing materials in an open center. Encourage the children to create many different jars by varying the levels of water in each. As they compose songs that they enjoy, they can record the notation and add their composition to a class book of music. Invite the children to think of other ways they can make music (for example, making instruments from recycled materials). Provide time for the children to experiment with playing new instruments and recording the code in different ways. The children can perform for an audience (parents, administration, or another class) using their new instruments or record their performances using technology and share their work beyond the classroom using social media. ■

## Roll a Piece of Art

**Materials:** wooden blocks, markers, paper

**Instructions:** Dedicate each block to a different element of design, one with the names of colors listed on each side and different types of lines on the other. Ensure that you have markers that match each color included on the block. Demonstrate how both blocks can be rolled at the same time. Using the results of what was rolled, draw a corresponding line on the paper. For example, if the color red and a zigzag line were the rolling results, you would then draw a red zigzag all over the paper. Continue rolling and drawing until the paper is filled with colorful overlapping lines.

*Roll the dice and draw the corresponding color and line on the paper until a beautiful piece of art emerges.*

**Observations:** Are the children able to read the color words, or do these need to be modified by using a color dot instead? Are they able to replicate the types of lines on their papers, or are these too complex? If the activity is too easy, would adding another die differentiate it? What other suggestions do the children have for the types of art they can create? How else might the children suggest using the dice?

**Next Steps:** Once the children understand the concept of how they can use the dice to code a piece of artwork, encourage them to change the elements on the dice (perhaps try shapes next), or add a die with pips. The children can roll and record what they see—if a triangle, the color blue, and the number 3 are rolled, then they draw three blue triangles on the paper. Encourage them to roll multiple sets of dice and create collaborative art using a large piece of butcher paper. Place the activity at a center for the children to visit and create at their leisure during activity time. ■

Children love to create potions and other interesting concoctions. In our classroom, the children were always mixing and matching shades of paint in their explorations. They loved to dip their brushes into various combinations of colors to see what magical shade would emerge as they mixed and stirred the paint on their paper. I found I was able to use this natural curiosity to help children code colors for one another that could be created and incorporated into their artwork.

## Color-Mixing Algorithms

**Materials:** various colors of paint (red, yellow, blue, white, black), cups, droppers, tablespoons, wooden sticks, chart paper, markers

**Instructions:** Remind the children that algorithms are like recipes, with step-by-step directions to follow to achieve an end result. Encourage them to consider what they know about color mixing (like primary shades mixing to form secondary colors, white lightening a color and black darkening it) and use this knowledge to write color algorithms for displaying in the art center. At first model for the children how two colors can be added together to form a new color. For example, if you add 5 tablespoons of blue paint to 5 tablespoons of yellow paint and stir, the result will be vibrant green. Next tell the children that displaying color algorithms in the art center will help everyone create interesting shades. As new shades are made, write them on the master color list. Invite the children to help write a color algorithm for the modeled color creation of vibrant green. Remind them to include as much detail as possible. Once the algorithm is written, use new materials and follow the steps to see if they were written clearly enough. The children can work in small groups at the art center to continue to create new shades and record the algorithms to include on the master color list. Give the new shades creative and interesting names to inspire the children to think more deeply about the experience and have ownership over the colors they create.

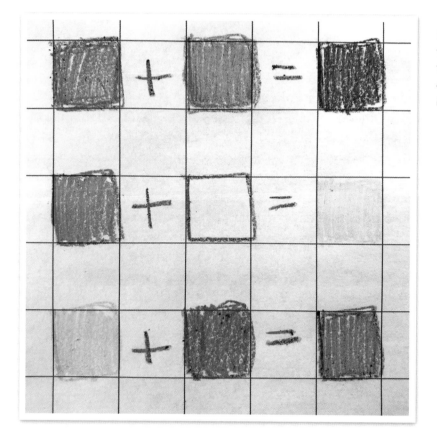

Different combinations of colors and their resulting shades are represented on paper.

**Observations:** Do the children have background knowledge regarding color mixing? Can they apply their knowledge of colors to create new shades? How clearly do the children verbally express the directions for creating their new color? When recording their directions, are the children clear and succinct? Do the instructions make sense?

**Next Steps:** Place the art materials at a table in the art center and encourage the children to visit during free-choice time and create and name their own unique colors. They can add the colors to the master color list over time. This same activity can be replicated with water tinted with food coloring and transported into clear containers using pipettes. Create algorithms to describe the new shades of water in a similar way. ■

Children can create transient art, art that is destined to be enjoyed for a short period of time, using loose parts. Transient art offers rich learning opportunities for the artist, who is not creating with an audience in mind but rather for the pleasure of the process. Once created it is not kept permanently but viewed quickly by onlookers and passersby before it is deconstructed into something else. Taking photos can help preserve transient art or allow the artist to later reflect on the art, similar to the following activity incorporating pattern blocks.

Pattern blocks are an excellent math manipulative to use with children to help them physically and visually explore and manipulate patterns. Pattern-block activities promote rich spatial thinking and logic in children. Tessellations relate to coding because they are reminiscent of digital artwork that incorporates enlarged pixels as part of the design process.

When children are encouraged to create designs with various lines of symmetry (horizontal, vertical, diagonal), they must consider how the blocks relate to one another and as small parts of a larger design. When children are comfortable creating symmetrical pictures, encourage them to create a design that uses rotational symmetry. The act of repeating the same section of blocks over and over as one works around in a circular motion not only infuses complex spatial thinking and problem-solving but also reinforces the idea of looping as the blocks are repeated in a specific way. Encourage them to deconstruct their tessellation, identifying the core of their pattern and articulating the coding rule for how many times it is looped in the design. Cores can also be isolated—take a photo of just the core and encourage the children to use it as a visual prompt for creating an entire tessellation.

## Pattern-Block Tessellations

**Materials:** flat working space, large collection of pattern block pieces, printed photos of tessellations (can be found using an online search)

**Instructions:** Encourage the children to explore creating as many different designs as possible using a variety of pattern blocks. They can work independently or together to create one incredibly large tessellation!

**Observations:** Are the children able to manipulate the pieces together strategically? Is there thought behind the placement of each piece, or is the child creating randomly? Can the child fit the pieces together so that no space is left in between; or if there is space remaining, is it purposeful to the aesthetics and design of the tessellation? Can the children identify the attributes of their patterns? Are they able to create accurate symmetrical designs? Can more challenging lines of symmetry, including diagonal and rotational, be explored

A complex tessellation is created by arranging wooden pattern blocks.

successfully? Are the children able to articulate the core of their tessellation? Are the children interested in taking photos of their work and using these as picture prompts for others to explore and re-create? What else can the children use the blocks for in their free explorations?

**Next Steps:** Offer the children a basket of pattern blocks on a large working surface during free-choice time. Encourage them to leave their uncompleted tessellations out (instead of tidying up when they are done working) for others to explore and continue working on. Take photos of the children's creations and add them to a tessellation book that documents their work over time. Review past tessellation work with the children and ask them to observe and reflect on how their previous work compares to their current work. ∎

## Pixel Pictures

**Materials:** large piece of grid paper, crayons or markers, samples of pixelated pictures (easily obtained from online searches)

**Instructions:** A bitmap is an image file that can be used to create computer graphics. Computer graphics become pixelated when a bitmap is displayed at such a very large size that it reveals individual pixels, which are the small single-colored squares that comprise the bitmap. Lead the children in a discussion about what bitmaps and pixels are. Show them a computer or tablet screen so they can see a real example. Display the sample pixelated pictures one at a time, and ask the children to share their thoughts regarding what they see in a large-group discussion. Question the children to dig more deeply into their thinking: What is the picture supposed to be? How do you know this? What shapes and colors are predominant in the picture? What does the picture remind you of? Show the children a large piece of grid paper. Using different colors of markers or crayons, begin filling in each square on the grid, one at a time, until a form or picture becomes evident. Ask the children to predict what you are drawing. Think aloud as you draw so that the children can understand the process you are following to create your own pixelated picture. Some children may benefit from reproducing a printed pixelated picture onto grid paper before creating their own. When they appear comfortable, provide individual grid paper and encourage them to experiment with creating their own pixelated pictures.

A child draws a pixelated picture of his house using crayons and grid paper.

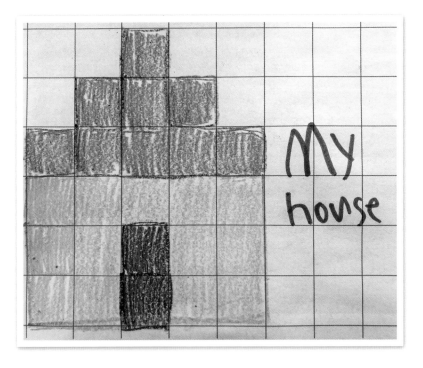

**Observations:** Are the children able to make reasonable predictions about what the original images were before becoming pixelated? Can they identify aspects of the pictures, including shapes, patterns, or colors? Are they interested in attempting to create their own pixelated art? Do they have an idea of what they'd like to represent on the grid paper, or are they experimenting by coloring in random squares? Are their pictures identifiable?

**Next Steps:** The children may enjoy working on this activity in pairs or small groups. Experience discussing and identifying pixelated pictures will help support children. For those children who require more practice, consider printing a variety of pixelated photos and encouraging them to observe the details closely and engage in discussions with peers regarding what the original images might have been. ∎

If the arts are a language of communication, helping children clearly articulate their ideas to others and encouraging them to actively listen and comprehend the messages being shared are incredibly important aspects of the creative process. The following activities use coding as a language of expression and rely on strong oral communication among children in order to be successful. They help children transcribe their oral coding ideas into tangible binary language using artistic materials as a visual representation, turning the abstract into something malleable.

## Follow-the-Leader Grid Art

**Materials:** multiple copies of large grid paper (the number of squares inside the grid depends on your students, as fewer squares make the game easier and more make it more challenging), markers

**Instructions:** Model the activity for the children before playing. Choose a child to play the game with you. Post the player's grid where the other children can see it. Keep your own copy hidden from view, perhaps on a clipboard on your lap. Determine a starting position with the other player, ensuring that the same spot is marked on both papers. Give directions to the player, one at a time, and encourage them to follow your instructions precisely. The instructions will tell the player where to move on the grid and what colors to fill in specific squares. For example, you might give these directions: "Begin at the start spot. Move right two spaces, move down three spaces, move left one space. Color that square red. Now move up five spaces, move left seven spaces. Color that square green." Give enough directions so that multiple places on the grid are colored. When the game is done, reveal your grid by placing it next to the player's grid. The goal is for both grids to match, indicating that the drawing code was successfully given and received. If there are differences, see where the errors were made and discuss how to debug the grid art so that they both match.

**Observations:** Is the player able to successfully pick the starting location? Is the player actively listening to the directions and successfully following them? If the activity is too easy, would increasing the number of squares in the grid differentiate it? What other materials can the children use to decorate the grid?

**Next Steps:** Once the activity is modeled, provide each child their own grid and set of markers. Repeat the activity again, this time leading the entire group in a game from your place at the front of the carpet. Ensure that each child has the correct starting position, then engage the group in creating a piece of grid art by giving a series of directions. When you are finished, reveal your master copy of code and ask the children if theirs is a match. Debug any mistakes. Pair children off and encourage them to play together at the carpet, with one child as the coder and the other as the player. Place the materials at a center for the children to use during free-choice activity time.  ■

## ASCII Beading Codes

**Materials:** ASCII binary codes, large collection of two different kinds of pony beads, pipe cleaners, index cards

**Instructions:** Explain to the children that ASCII (American Standard Code for Information Interchange) is the code that computers use to understand text (IBM Knowledge Center 2019). Each **binary code** is a string of bits using the numbers 0 and 1 in different orders. Bits are the individual characters in binary code. Display the binary code templates for the children and highlight different letters as examples. The children will be able to see that each letter has two codes, one to represent uppercase and another for lowercase. Invite the children to help you write a specific word using the ASCII code. In this activity, the number 0 can be represented by one color (like blue pony beads), and the number 1 can be represented by another color (like white pony beads). Model for the children how you can spell a word using binary code by first finding the letters on the chart and then representing the number sequence with the corresponding number of pony beads. Each word will require many beads in order to be completed. For example, if I were to spell my name, Deanna, in binary code, it would require forty-eight beads.

Invite the children to code a word together with you. Names and their corresponding code can be written on large chart paper for reference. During free-choice time, invite the children to visit a table where they can translate their names (or other short words and phrases, like "mom," "dad," or "I love you") into binary code by placing the corresponding order and number of beads on a pipe cleaner. If there are too many beads, link multiple pipe cleaners together, or the children can string the beads on a longer piece of yarn. These coded messages can be worn as bracelets or necklaces.

**Observations:** Binary coding might be a difficult concept for some children to understand at first because it is a lengthy and abstract representation of written

language. Do the children seem interested and engaged in the experience? Are their fingers able to manipulate the small beads? Are they able to locate letters and their corresponding code on the chart? Can they track the numbers used in long codes and transfer these into written words using just the numbers? Are they able to follow along without losing track as beads are added to the pipe cleaner? What are their reactions if they do lose track in the code? What strategies do the children use to organize information in this experience? What do they do when they have made an error and need to self-correct?

**Next Steps:** If the children are interested in this experience, they can continue to create coded jewelry using a variety of bead colors. The bracelets can be gifted to family members and friends for special holidays and events. The children can be encouraged to write different words on index cards (one word per card) and create a binary dictionary for easy reference when familiar words and phrases need to be spelled. Add these to a book or place them on a ring for easy access. Encourage the children to create alternative symbols for each upper- and lowercase alphabet letter, and use these to create secret codes for one another to solve. ■

## Pool Noodle Binary Codes

**Materials:** binary code templates (printed and laminated), two pool noodles (different colors) cut into two-inch cookies with a slit through the middle, string

**Instructions:** This is a good way to bring the previous activity outside or adapt it for children who struggle with smaller materials like beads. Similar to the previous activity, explain to the children that ASCII is the code that computers use to understand text. Each binary code is a string of bits using the numbers 0 and 1 in different orders. Display the binary code templates to the children and highlight different letters as examples. They will be able to see that each letter has two codes, one to represent uppercase and another for lowercase. Invite the children to help you write a specific word in the ASCII code using the pool noodles. In this activity, represent the number 0 with one color (such as green noodle pieces) and the number 1 with another color (such as orange noodle pieces). Model for the children how you can spell a word using binary code by first finding the letters on the chart and then representing the letters using noodle pieces. The midway cut on each piece will help it slide onto the string. Practice coding different words with the children by asking for volunteers to identify the code for each letter and adding the pieces onto the string in the correct sequence.

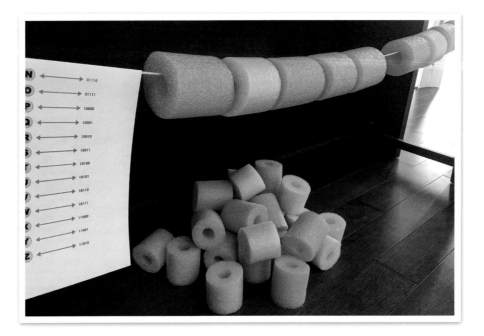

Different colors of pool noodle pieces represent binary code.

**Observations:** Are the children able to locate letters and their corresponding codes on the chart? Are they able to place the pool noodle piece on the string successfully? Can they track the numbers used in long codes and transfer these into written words using just the numbers? Are they able to follow along without losing track as pieces are added to the string? Do they persevere with this challenging task? What strategies do the children use to organize information in this experience or when they have made an error and need to self-correct?

**Next Steps:** This activity would be ideal as an outdoor coding experience. Hang the string between trees or along a fence and place a large collection of pool noodle pieces in a basket next to the string. Hang the ASCII charts nearby as well. The children can create their own code or attempt to decipher code left on the string by someone else. ■

Big-body creative coding incorporates active play using children's gross-motor muscles and capitalizes on their intrinsic need to explore using their whole bodies. Physical play in the gym or during recess or outdoor play is a perfect time to infuse activities with computational thinking. Umaschi Bers (2018) reminds us that coding activities that are physical and game-like in nature often encourage reluctant children to engage in the coding experience because the activities are enjoyable and usually framed with a playful problem to solve. The following activities are meant for very large spaces where children are free to run and jump without inhibition or fear. Large coding grids can be easily made using chalk or masking tape. Some schools have even painted grids directly on the playground surface, providing an instant and always accessible space for children to incorporate into organized activities and free-choice explorations of their own creation.

## Coding Players on a Large Grid

**Materials:** large coding grid, dry-erase board, dry-erase markers

**Instructions:** This game is for two players, but you may want to model the activity for the children before offering it during free-choice time. One child is the coder, and the other is the player. Determine a starting and ending position. The coder prompts the player to move around the grid by giving oral directions and recording these on the dry-erase board ("Move forward one space. Turn left. Move left three spaces."). The player follows the directions exactly as given by the coder. If mistakes are made, the players work together to debug the problem. The goal is to help the player reach the end location.

**Observations:** Are the children able to give each other clear and efficient directions? Can their coding sequences be transcribed accurately onto the dry-erase board? Can the children follow directions? What other ideas might they have for enhancing this experience and turning it into a game? Can props be added to enhance the experience?

**Next Steps:** Add obstacles to the grid that players need to maneuver to add complexity to the coding directions. This game can also be turned into a coding race. Children can work in teams of two. Each team takes a turn coding the player from start to finish on the grid. Teams cannot have players on the same square at the same time. See who can reach the end location the fastest or using the least number of coding directions. ■

## Outdoor Coding Card Lines

**Materials:** blank coding cards, markers, string, clothespins

**Instructions:** Hang the string between two trees or posts and offer blank coding cards to the children. Encourage them to consider a favored outdoor activity and help code their friends through the experience. For example, if they want to code their friends through the experience of making a sandcastle in the sandbox, they would draw pictures of each step that needed to be followed, one step per card. As the cards are created, hang them in order on a string near where the sand is located. The children can guide one another through complex outdoor activities by creating and then following the algorithm.

Coding instructions can easily be displayed outdoors by folding cards in half and hanging them on a line suspended between two trees.

**Observations:** What activities do the children seem interested in coding? What activities are they having difficulty performing that coding cards might assist with? Are they interested in creating the coding cards? What other ideas do the children have for using the coding cards in their play?

**Next Steps:** Use coding card lines to explore and represent other cyclical events observed in nature. For example, if the children discover a nest, they can code the life cycle of a bird and hang the coding cards near where the nest was found. Laminate the coding cards to withstand the elements if they're left outdoors for long periods of time. Bring the coding card lines inside the classroom as a visual aid at different learning centers or in daily routines (like the process of properly washing your hands, a game that can be played in the water table). ■

## Obstacle Course Coding

**Materials:** blank coding cards, markers, string, clothespins, outdoor play equipment, large loose parts (stumps, logs, balls, wooden spools)

**Instructions:** Encourage the children to plan out a lengthy obstacle course using the landscape and other outdoor features. Draw actions in the sequence on coding cards and hang them on the string, ordering the actions and providing a framework for participants to follow (for example, jumping on a stump, hopping over a log, or bouncing a ball five times). The children can guide the person traveling the course by following along with the sequence and calling out the actions. As the course is mastered, encourage the children to add more complex codes to the sequence to challenge users in different ways.

**Observations:** Are there enough diverse materials and features in the yard to challenge the children in the creation of their obstacle course? Are the children able to translate their ideas for physical activity into codes? Do the children properly sequence the cards? Can they follow the actions as outlined in their proper order? What other uses for the coding cards might the children have?

**Next Steps:** Bring the coding cards into the gym as a visual aid for children to follow in different centers. The children can create their own complex sequences or use the cards to provide guidance and direction in games of their own devising. ■

## Hopscotch Coding

**Materials:** multiple sets of interlocking foam mats, permanent markers or sidewalk chalk

**Instructions:** Designate two mats as the starting and ending points, and label them "start" and "end." Divide the remaining mats in half. On one group, draw large directional arrows. On the other group, write different prompts for physical actions (*jump, clap, stomp, twirl*). Printed actions on paper can also be taped on each mat so actions can be easily changed on a regular basis. Arrange the foam mats in a varied pathway and model for the children how they can move along following the direction of the arrows and stopping on each action prompt to perform what the direction requires. Control structures such as loops can also be included to make the path more complex. After modeling how the activity works, change the sequence of the mats and ask a volunteer to follow the sequence in the new order. Place the mats in a large bin and make them available to the children during free-choice activity time in the classroom or gym, or as an outdoor learning center.

Add instructions to each foam piece by writing on it using sidewalk chalk. The chalk is easily washed off, so different instructions can be written in future experiences.

**Observations:** Do the children understand how the pathway works? Are they able to decipher the action mats and follow through on the required movements? Can they be challenged with complex control structures to differentiate the task?

**Next Steps:** Provide blank mats for the children to draw their own action prompts. Encourage them to assemble the mats in different pathways and code one another through various physical sequences. The children can document their friends' attempts by using the class tablet. They can lengthen or shorten the path depending on the level of difficulty required. ∎

## Sidewalk Coding

**Materials:** paper, writing materials including pencils and markers, large sidewalk, sidewalk chalk

**Instructions:** Remind the children that code can be a symbol of representation for actions or movements. Model for them how an outdoor sidewalk obstacle course can be planned ahead of time on paper. Brainstorm together with the children various activities they would like included in the obstacle course (such as hop on one foot, twirl, jump, spin) and decide on symbols to represent these. You can also create an action legend as a visual aid. Once the course is drawn on paper as a code, head outdoors together and transfer the code from paper to sidewalk using chalk. When complete, demonstrate for the children how to use

Instructions for children to follow can be written on a sidewalk using chalk.

the symbols as code and move through the course by following the sequence in the proper order. The children can take turns exploring the course together. Replicate the course many times so that multiple children can experience it at once, or race each other to see who can complete it the fastest.

**Observations:** Are the children able to transfer their ideas for physical actions to symbols on paper? Do they understand that the paper coding is a representation for the larger scaled one to be drawn using sidewalk chalk? Can they correctly follow the sequence outlined using chalk? What other ideas do they wish to incorporate into their sequences? What other games are they interested in playing using the code?

**Next Steps:** Encourage the children to plan and design their own obstacle courses on paper. Remind them to include a legend to explain their coding sequence. Bring the children outside and help them draw their own obstacle courses, taking time afterward to try out each one. ■

## Collect-the-Parts Race (Snowman Hunt)

**Materials:** large coding grid, dry-erase board, dry-erase markers, loose parts for the activity (for example, if making a snowman, you need a hat, scarf, carrot nose, buttons, sticks, and so on), basket

**Instructions:** This game is for two players, but you may want to model the activity for the children before offering it during free-choice time. One child is the coder, and the other is the player. Determine a starting and ending position. The coder prompts the player to move around the grid by giving oral directions and recording these on the dry-erase board ( "Move forward one space. Turn left. Move left three spaces."). The purpose is to lead the player to each of the snowman parts so they can be collected and placed in the basket for use later on when making a snowman. The player follows the directions exactly as given by the coder. If mistakes are made, the players work together to debug the problem. The goal is to help the player reach the end location after collecting all of the snowman parts. Substitute the snowman parts for other props depending on what type of inquiry your students are currently interested in.

**Observations:** Are the children able to give each other clear and efficient directions? Can their coding sequences be transcribed accurately onto the dry-erase board? Can the children follow directions? What other ideas might they have for enhancing this experience and turning it into a game? Are the children able to gather all needed props?

**Next Steps:** Add obstacles to the grid that players need to maneuver to add complexity to the coding directions. This game can also be turned into a coding race. The children can work in teams of two, and each team takes a turn coding the player from start to finish on the grid. Teams cannot have players on the same square at the same time. See who can pick up the most parts needed for the snowman first. ∎

## Creative Coding

Creative expression is a motivating and engaging way for children to explore a variety of developmental areas and domains. Integrating subjects helps educators fulfill multiple curriculum requirements at once. Children can use aesthetic unplugged coding activities to communicate symbolically in a variety of ways.

# CHAPTER 7

# Coding to Support Literacy

*Mother's Day was filled with sunshine, laughter, and the usual mess of having the kids home for two days in a row, roaming indoors and out and savoring the freedom that unstructured time provides. However, this weekend was also the first time my son Caleb, age seven, expressed an interest in learning how to use the elastic-band loom that had been sitting in his closet since December. Early Saturday morning, I noticed him watching his sister, Cadence, work from afar. He eventually made his way to her side and spent several minutes observing her. Was it hard? Could he borrow her stuff? Did she have extra elastics for him too? Would she help him if he got stuck? He peppered her with questions. She timed her answers to the crescendo of video clips as she worked on her Ninja Turtle design while following an online tutorial. And then something caught his eye in the corner of her screen. He was sold. There, in bright red and yellow, was the most comical-looking elastic-y hotdog. And with that he was off to gather his loom and iPad and set to work on the kitchen table.*

*After an hour or so, I heard him set his hook down with a clatter. I approached him to see how it was going.*

*"Terrible!" he responded. "The girl in this video doesn't give clear directions. I have no clue what to do. She's not making any sense."*

In the past, I have spent much time linking coding to math due to the rich, integrated opportunities for number sense and geometry it provides. But what about literacy? Many educators are continuously looking at ways to embed and improve meaningful language-based activities in their emergent programs. To experience success in a task, clear, concise, and direct instructions are critical. Reflect on your literacy program and consider areas of student interest and need using these reflective prompts:

> ❯ What is your biggest area of concern regarding children's language learning?

> ❯ How are you supplementing classroom activities to provide meaningful frameworks that both encourage and guide children?

> ❯ Can computational thinking help with this?

> How does coding encourage users to become more proficient communicators?

> Can coding support a transition from oral language to reading and writing for children?

> Can coding strengthen children's literacy programs in the same ways it does math?

I believe that young children who use complex, integrated coding activities in their daily lives will have opportunities to strengthen their literacy skills in many versatile and complex ways.

According to Umaschi Bers (2018), coding is "the new literacy," helping children think aloud and express themselves to be understood by others, even those not in close physical proximity (24). Coding can be written as a language by a child who wants to share their thinking far beyond the confines of their immediate environment. In Reggio Emilia, reading and writing are considered some of the hundreds of languages that children use to explore, represent, and communicate their understandings of the world around them (Wein 2008, 2014; Wurm 2005). This communication can be intricate and beautiful in the same way a letter to a friend or a short story can express sentiment and emotion. This written artifact can be read, revised, and altered by someone else in a shareable format, such as a coding algorithm. When my daughter was eleven, she loved visiting the Scratch website (www.scratch.mit.edu), where she could access millions of programs created by other children from around the world and look inside to see each of their codes. She thought it was amazing that someone from across the world was able to communicate a message to her and that she could understand it. She could then modify the code and share it back, and the two could become digital pen pals. Coding allows a programmer to infuse intention and emotion in their specific message to others. Coding also empowers children to become literate in the twenty-first century, preparing them for life in an unknown future. The language must be appropriate for the developmental stage and abilities of the learner. Therefore, for the purposes of this book, I am referring to representation in unplugged coding including the oral language and symbolic representation that children use for their specific needs (such as arrows or pictures). As children become more confident and able, they can continue to explore more complex coding languages in subsequent lessons and activities.

As with reading and writing, children who work within the language of coding are at different levels of comprehension and fluency, each using a different tool for personal expression and communication to a greater audience. I've observed many children over the years fearful to take risks in their reading and writing using the English language, scared to make errors as they communicate in a printed format or attempt to read the ideas of others. They felt their language had to be perfectly presented if they were committing the ideas to a permanent written representation. Pencil-and-paper tasks can be scary for young learners! Consider the Reggio Emilia belief that children are capable and creative beings, and all children can thrive if given the individual time and support they require. These same children have thrived in unplugged activities. Communicating using the language of coding appeared to be different, as these children were not afraid to take risks in their explorations and experiment with representing ideas symbolically. They felt free to take risks and try new things, knowing that mistakes were bugs that could easily be fixed.

Over time I've realized that in addition to empowering children to be confident communicators using symbolic language, coding promotes language across our program in a variety of ways. Considering each of these has helped me realize just how literacy-rich unplugged coding can be and how it can complement all aspects of the curriculum. Coding enhances literacy in many ways:

> **Coding requires clear and accurate language.** Computers follow the code outlined in their programs. There is no room for interpretation, and as a result, programmers must be incredibly clear and detailed in their algorithms. When children use coding as a language of communication in the classroom, they practice this succinct way of articulating directions to others on a regular basis. Over time they will improve in their ability to be precise when crafting these programs and directing others in activities.

> **Coding reinforces concepts of print.** In our classroom, children are encouraged to write their code in different ways. They can order our class set of coding cards on the floor or in a pocket chart, or they can write their directions using a series of predetermined symbols (such as an arrow or stop sign). When writing or reading these directions, they are encouraged to move from top to bottom and left to right, replicating the way we read and write in the English language. I always ask them to use their reading finger and point to each card as they work. This reinforces the same concepts of print we are working on in our whole- and small-group literacy activities.

> **Coding uses symbolic language.** Because early coding incorporates pictures, many children can easily create messages for one another by sequencing coding cards or drawing established symbols digitally or on paper. A class can determine its own set of symbols before coding work begins so that everyone understands what they represent. Over time and with experience, children will become proficient communicators with these. Just as early mark-making is a foundational part of establishing positive literacy behaviors, coding helps children easily communicate their

ideas to others, showing that oral language can be translated and preserved in multiple ways. Children will be able to read and write coding instructions symbolically even if they are not yet fluent using letter and sound relationships.

> **Coding builds confidence and fluency in early readers and writers.** With practice children will improve in their ability to communicate using symbolic language. In our classroom, coding activities are always very popular, and even the children who are most reluctant in more traditional literacy activities want to participate. This grows their mindset and confidence because the more they practice, the better they become.

> **Coding encourages active listening.** Regardless of how well constructed an algorithm is, it can only be successfully implemented if a child is listening intently and following through on the given directions. Coding work requires concentration and full engagement. This helps children practice being attentive and responsive listeners.

> **Coding is a universal language.** In our classroom, children blog and tweet extensively about their daily experiences. A very important part of the inquiry process is sharing one's understanding beyond the metaphorical walls of the classroom. Because coding is used all around the world (and is such a hot topic in education right now), children can participate in global events, communicating with children in different countries, even where English is not the common language. The Hour of Code event is a great motivator to give you a framework and timeline for implementing coding in the classroom and connecting with other like-minded educators.

> **Coding encourages sequencing.** In our classroom, children often use favorite texts as the foundation of their coding games (retelling the events in *The Gingerbread Man*, helping the Gingerbread Man escape the fox at the end of the story). Coding sequences a story from beginning to end, which requires users to group events together and retell them in the proper order. This means that children need to be able to accurately sequence a story so that it makes sense. They need to consider the beginning, middle, and end events and retell these in their coding directions so the game makes sense. This strengthens their comprehension of literature and encourages them to demonstrate their knowledge in hands-on ways as they play with stories.

> **Coding incorporates concepts of print.** Coding requires users to imagine setting, characters, and plot. This reinforces text comprehension, especially when favorite read-alouds are used as the inspiration behind activities. When creating their own stories using the coding board, children need to establish engaging characters and plots for the activities to be fun to play.

> **Coding is found in daily routines.** Thinking and communicating in algorithms extend beyond coding activities. Adults and children have multiple opportunities each day to give and receive directions. When we think as coders, we realize that we are more effective and efficient when our communication is clear and easy to follow. Children can be reminded of this in their work outside of programming. Educator Brian Aspinall emphasized at a recent professional development event I attended that he asks his students to "speak to each other in algorithms" in daily activities, even those unrelated to coding, to emphasize clear and direct language.

> **Coding is an expressive language.** Much like the arts, coding helps children articulate their ideas and demonstrate their comprehension to others. Emergent programs influenced by Reggio Emilia encourage children to explore and share their learning using hundreds of languages, including the arts, physical expression, and building. Coding can become another language children use to communicate in inquiry-based classrooms, especially once they are proficient in using it on a regular basis. For example, why not encourage a child to demonstrate their understanding by creating a code to tell a story and show and share their new knowledge with others?

## Children as Communicators

Children are born to communicate and interact socially with the world around them. From their first cries and gestures as infants to their growing ability to use words and then short phrases as toddlers, they are curious about their surroundings and eager to engage fully with their caregivers (Dietze and Kashin 2018). Constructivist classrooms are social, and successful learning occurs through relationships and knowledge-building with adults and peers. Oral language develops naturally over time as children are exposed to positive models of language and develop and practice these in immersive, supportive, and print-rich learning environments. Playful learning situations such as coding can support children's language and literacy development in many ways (Umaschi Bers 2018). In addition to serving as a motivating scenario for using language in a real-life context, interactive games and experiences can help children symbolically express the ideas and intentions behind their actions. Children learn and use new vocabulary in relevant and meaningful scenarios while building their schema regarding content area. Oral language is the system through which children use spoken words to express their feelings, ideas, and knowledge and make connections to the world around them. This becomes the foundation for future listening, speaking, reading, and writing work for a number of reasons:

> Oral language develops children's word repertoire as they learn the pronunciation and meaning behind words used in conversations with others, building a robust vocabulary that will lead to more informed reading comprehension.

> Oral-language practice builds children's understanding of word and sentence structures so children who can clearly articulate their thoughts to others are better able to translate these to written representations in later experiences.

> Oral-language acquisition increases children's confidence in communicating for a wide audience and builds intrinsic motivation for continued development in listening, reading, and writing.

There are many ways in which unplugged coding activities promote active listening and clear oral communication in children (Umaschi Bers 2018). In these experiences, children become computational conversationalists, sharing their ideas orally and symbolically with others for a specific purpose. Each child has unique ideas and opinions to add to enhance the collective conversations occurring in the classroom. Adults can model proper vocabulary and directions, supporting children's increasing comfort and complexity within the activities. Unplugged coding requires that children interact with other children, resulting in rich peer learning. Less-experienced children will gain valuable computational language and skills from others, and coding mentors will reinforce and heighten positive habits of speech in their work leading others. There are also many opportunities for children to transfer their oral directions to a pictorial or symbolic format, helping them see the relationship between speech and writing by encouraging a type of coding storytelling through oral and written formats.

I believe that any activity in this book promotes oral language though the use of clear and succinct directions and active listening. However, the following activities have been used in our classroom specifically to promote oral-language development in children while giving them additional experience with the process of coding. In many activities, I've also woven in curriculum expectations from other learning domains, making the activity more complex and meaningful for children. These activities are easily adaptable and can be incorporated into other areas of your program and routines.

## Coder Says, Robot Does

**Materials:** blank cards, markers, tape, easel

**Instructions:** This activity follows the template of the familiar childhood game Simon Says, and can be played in a large or small group. You can also modify by having the children practice in pairs. One person is the coder, and the rest of the players are the robots. The coder programs the robots through designated actions by giving a command with the word *robot* preceding the action. For example, if the coder wants the robots to jump five times in a row, they would say, "Robots, please jump five times." The robots first listen to the directions and then perform the actions. The coder can create increasingly complex directions by adding to their sequence ("Robots, please jump five times and touch your toes twice," "Robots, please jump five times, touch your toes twice, and spin once"). The robots must listen carefully to the directions and follow through in sequence. You can ask the children for suggestions on rules to make the game more complex. Maybe they'd like to add controls so that if the word *please* is not used by the coder, the robots do not follow through on the directions ("Robots, touch your toes" would result in no action from the robots, but "Robots, *please* touch your toes" would). Maybe the children want to have responses for robots who have bugs in their codes and make mistakes in their actions (the coder must take their place, or the actions are repeated again by the entire group until they are performed in the correct sequence). The promotion of a safe and supportive space is most important, so keep that in mind if imposing certain rules for sequences performed out of place. You know your group best.

**Observations:** Are the children able to give clear directions to one another? Can they follow simple directions and perform the actions correctly? What happens when more complex sequences are added? Can they retain and recall the sequence? What suggestions do the children offer for improving the experience of the game? Are the children able to give and receive directions more effectively in whole- or small-group experiences? Does paired work (one coder and one robot) give them more opportunities for success?

**Next Steps:** Many children benefit from having a visual cue to support them in following a complex sequence. Encourage the coder to draw a picture of the action or write the action word and display these in sequence by taping them in order on an easel. If the children have difficulties drawing or writing quickly, consider having prewritten words or photos of children performing the actions for instant use. Consider encouraging more physical actions when playing the game in the gym or during outdoor time. ■

## Coding with Sequencing Cards

**Materials:** large collection of purchased or premade sequencing picture cards (such as how to brush your teeth or how to make a sandwich), pocket chart

**Instructions:** Sit the children in a large circle or around a large table and spread the cards randomly in the middle space. Encourage the children to work together to arrange a series of picture cards in the logical sequences to create the story from beginning to end to demonstrate and reinforce their recollection of an experience. As each sequence is identified, add them in order to the pocket chart for display. Encourage the children to use the words *beginning, middle,* and *end* or *first, then, next,* and *finally* to help describe the order of actions.

These three sequence cards show the order of how to brush your teeth.

**Observations:** Are the children able to decipher and isolate an activity after looking at a large collection of cards? Once they identify a potential activity, can they locate all the cards that belong to the sequence? Can they accurately order the cards from beginning to end? Do they use appropriate terminology when describing the actions in each step? Can they self-correct or notice errors in the sequences of others and work toward fixing these?

**Next Steps:** Invite the children to think about daily routines or enjoyable activities and create their own sequences by drawing pictures on blank cards. Once they have created a sequence, laminate their cards and place them at a retell center for other children to explore during free-choice time. Differentiate the activity by encouraging the children to create simple (three cards) or complex sequences (four or more cards). The children can also add words or sentences to their cards to help describe the action occurring on each.  ■

## First, Then, Next, Finally

**Materials:** familiar story, markers, storytelling boxes

**Instructions:** This task helps children break a larger story into smaller parts for retell. After reading a familiar book to the children, encourage them to deconstruct it by using the prompts "first, next, then, finally." These match the order of the story and are helpful prompts for considering how the action unfolded through simple retell (First the prince was kidnapped by a dragon, then the princess discovered where he was hiding, next she tricked the dragon into doing so much exercise he fell asleep, and finally she rescued the prince so he was free). As the children deconstruct the story and describe it in four parts, encourage them to draw a pictorial representation in each story box to represent what they are saying. Once the drawings are complete, the children can use them to retell the story in a simple picture sequence.

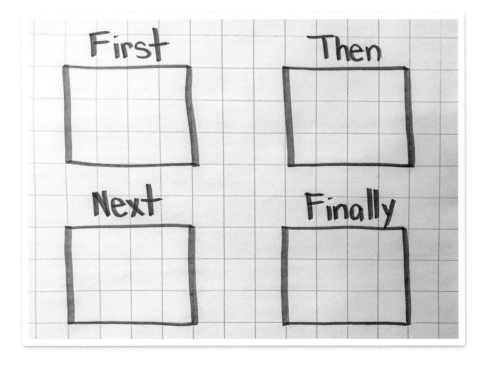

*Children can draw pictures in the template to sequence four parts of a story.*

**Observations:** Are the children able to retell the story in segmented retell by highlighting the main parts of the story line? Do they depict important events describing the beginning, middle, and end of the text? Can they identify the characters and setting to enhance their pictures? Do they include pertinent details, or do they focus on elements of the story that aren't as important?

**Next Steps:** Provide large copies of blank storytelling boxes for the children to use at the writing center. Encourage them to retell familiar stories. Children who are ready can also add sentences below each box to describe what is happening in each. In addition to books, the children can use storytelling boxes to describe routines that occur in the classroom (such as hand washing). Laminate and hang these in the appropriate place in the classroom and use them as visual aids to support children in their work in that area. ∎

## Routine Retell Algorithm

**Materials:** markers, chart paper, photos

**Instructions:** Algorithms put a story together, while modularity takes it apart. When children realize that different parts of their programs can be separated to perform separate tasks, that is called modularity. This is basically when a larger story or event is chunked into small sections (for example, the act of getting ready for school can be broken down into small parts: waking up, getting out of bed, using the bathroom, washing hands, brushing teeth, and so forth). Each section is an act in itself, but put together they form a larger task or story. Encourage the children to think about a classroom routine (such as morning entry or lunchtime) or any other activity they might need support with. Challenge the children to talk through the various steps of the routine in its proper order (Walk through the classroom door, put the backpack on the floor, take off your coat, hang the coat in a cubby). As the children describe the sequence of events, record their ideas in order on the chart paper. Once they are satisfied that they've included all steps in the sequence, ask a volunteer to dramatize the algorithm from start to finish. This may mean moving to a different part of the classroom, depending on where the routine takes place. As the child acts out each step, refer to the written algorithm and ask the children to consider if they've included each action in the proper order. If steps were omitted, add these to the algorithm. Continue role-playing and revising until the children are satisfied they have created an accurate retell for the routine being explored.

**Observations:** Are the children able to deconstruct routines into segmented activities that form an entire sequence when conducted together? Do they clearly articulate each step? Are they able to accurately recall each act that composes the larger action or routine? Are the children able to act out the algorithm and recognize when mistakes have been made or important pieces missed?

*The order of how to dress for winter weather is written for children to follow.*

**Next Steps:** Differentiate the task, and ask the children to write codes for easier or more complex tasks, depending on their abilities. Challenge the children to draw pictures to represent their own codes for other parts of their day using storytelling boxes. Consider taking photos of the children in action, and post them in a prominent area to help with future classroom work (for example, a winter sequence could be created to support children when getting dressed in snowsuits for outdoor play, providing a visual for the order in which each piece of clothing should be placed on the body). ■

## Directional Arrows in Dramatic Playscapes

**Materials:** flat river rocks, permanent markers, storytelling props, sand table

**Instructions:** Draw one large arrow on each river rock with permanent marker and let dry. Observe the children as they play in the sensory table and notice if a story line with a clear beginning, middle, and end is developing. Engage the children in a conversation about what they are playing to make visible the progression of their plot. Once the children become comfortable with the retell, place the arrow stones in order from start to finish. For example, if the children are role-playing with toy dinosaurs in the sand table and create a story where one dinosaur chases another (starting in one corner, across the sand, around a large rock, over the path, and under a tree), place the arrows facing in that direction to describe the movement or story of the dinosaurs' actions and help children see the path of their play. Once the arrows are placed in order, the children can retrace the dinosaurs' steps again with the toys or create new narratives for the characters to follow.

*Stones with arrows help show the path the dinosaur takes through the playscape.*

**Observations:** Do the children tell a story with a beginning, middle, and end in their imaginary play? Are they interested in recording or retelling the story using arrow stones? Once the arrows are placed, can the children use them to retell their story? Are the children interested in modifying or innovating their story and moving the arrows accordingly?

**Next Steps:** Offer the arrow stones in a basket near your sensory or building centers. Encourage the children to incorporate them whenever they are role-playing or retelling a story with play props like toys and loose parts. ∎

## Pattern Block Barrier Game

**Materials:** box or cardboard barriers, placemats, large collection of pattern blocks

**Instructions:** This activity is best for a small group of children. Sit together with the children around the table, each person hiding their design from the others by working on top of a placement and behind a barrier. Give each child a large collection of pattern blocks. In the role of the coder, give the children one direction at a time to place their blocks in a specific location on the placemat ("Place the orange square in the middle," "Place one green triangle on top so that the point is up," and so forth). As you give directions, ensure you are also placing the blocks on your own mat. Once you have finished describing your creation, remove your barrier and ask the children to do the same. Compare your pattern block design to those of the children to see whether they were able to follow the directions successfully. Clear the mats and assign a new coder. Repeat the process.

A wooden barrier separates the two playing areas in this game.

**Observations:** Do the children know the correct names of the pattern blocks? Do they appear comfortable following directions, or are they getting frustrated easily? Is the coder pacing their directions so they can be easily understood and followed by others? Are the children experiencing success following the directions and creating replicas of the model?

**Next Steps:** This activity can also be performed using a variety of loose parts (such as felt pieces) to create a scene or tell a story. You can also remove the manipulatives and have the children draw what they are instructed by the coder ("Draw an orange circle in the middle of your paper. Color the inside yellow. On the right-hand side, draw a long rectangle."). ■

## Unifix Cube Creations

**Materials:** large collection of plastic linking cubes that snap together (such as Unifix cubes)

**Instructions:** Encourage the children to sit in a large circle on the carpet or around a table together. Give each child ten cubes. One person is the coder and gives the children one direction at a time to manipulate their cubes in a specific way. For example, the coder might say, "Get one cube. Put two cubes on top of it. Place another cube at the bottom of the stack and in front." As the coder gives the directions, they should also be making a cube structure that is out of sight of

A plastic cube creation made by a child.

the others to be displayed at the end of the experience. At first give the children very simple commands to ensure they are successful and understand the directions. As they get more practice, give more complex directions leading to more unique cube creations. When the coder is finished giving directions, hold the model structure up so that the children can compare and see if they successfully followed the directions. When the children are comfortable, encourage them to take turns coding their peers in cube creations.

**Observations:** Are the children able to use correct terminology to describe the placement of each cube? Do the children place their cubes in the correct location as directed by the coder? Do they persevere in this activity? Are they able to sustain attention and feel successful? Would it be more developmentally appropriate or easier for the children to create the cube structures in pairs or trios?

**Next Steps:** If the cube structures are too complex for your learners, consider adapting the activity so the children are creating a specific order of cubes by color (not necessarily a pattern). A coder might ask the children to start with a specific color of cube(s) and work from there ("Place two green cubes side by side. Put a blue cube in between the green cubes. Place a red cube at the right side of the line of cubes."). ■

Playful experiences support children in language acquisition, which builds the foundation they need for later reading and writing success. In addition to enriching children's oral language, one of the first ways that children are exposed to reading and writing is through exploring high-quality children's books. Being read to by an adult helps them make connections to pictures, print, and language, including comprehension and concepts of print. Storytelling is a major component of the coding work we have experienced in our classroom. It helps children connect socially and emotionally to rich texts and gives them purpose and motivation in their work of retelling these favorites or authoring their own. It also means that with each new inquiry, the books and resources children use can be translated into coding activities, providing opportunities for enhanced understanding. Educators can repeatedly use the same framework for activities but change them based on the topics and books being explored. According to Stadler and Ward (2005), children experience five levels when exploring and developing narratives:

1. Children **label** people and objects (like a character in a story).

2. Children **list** specific criteria (like a character's traits or actions).

3. Children **connect** a character to a central issue or theme (how the character connects to the overall story).

4. Children **sequence** events (describing the cause-and-effect actions of the character).

5. Children **narrate** a story (summarizing the information they have regarding the character and actions into a story with a beginning, middle, and end).

Children are storytellers, revisiting their favorite tales over and over. With each new retell, they use increasingly more complex vocabulary, improve their fluency and articulation, integrate rich gestures and intonation, and draw their audiences in. The blurring of reality and make-believe sparks imagination and inspires rich dramatic play in our classroom. As each story is told, children create mental pictures and internally play out the narrative, imagining nuances of characters, intricate details of settings, and complex emotions. Children connect texts to their own lives and the world around them, using previous experiences to build knowledge and become deeply invested in their realities. How do children build such layered background knowledge to help support them in future work?

Children often incorporate storytelling into unplugged coding activities. Whether they are retelling or innovating a favorite and familiar book or creating their own story with characters, settings, and a plot, they are using what they know about engaging books to capture their audience and immerse them into the storytelling experience. When children are reading and following coding directions, they use their understanding of concepts of print (for example, text moves left to right and up and down) to decode the message. They read the messages of others so they can follow through on a task. Their messages can be written and shared beyond the walls of the classroom, helping them bring their ideas beyond their community of learners. Throughout the coding experience, children make connections, engage in conversations, and plan future activities using their previous reading experiences as a foundation. I have used the following activities to encourage children to retell familiar stories and innovate their own.

## Life Cycle Sequence Coding

**Materials:** large collection of purchased or premade life cycle sequencing cards, string, clothespins

**Instructions:** Sit the children in a large circle or at a large table and spread the cards randomly in the middle space. Encourage the children to work together to arrange a series of picture cards in logical sequences to retell a life cycle from beginning to end to demonstrate and reinforce their understanding (such as egg, caterpillar, chrysalis, butterfly or baby, toddler, teen, adult, older adult). As each sequence is identified, put them in order and clip them on a string for display.

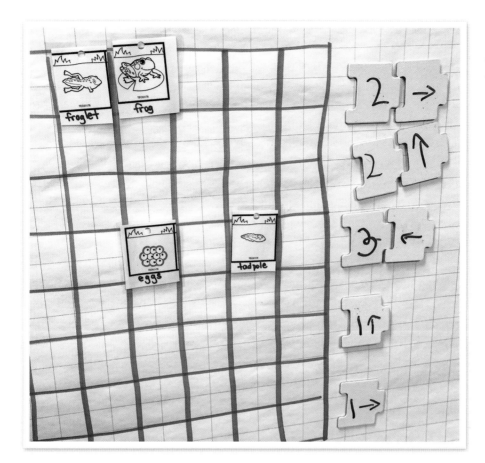

Directions code a path to each stage of the frog life cycle.

**Observations:** Are the children able to identify what is happening on each card? Can they orally identify and isolate a life cycle from the large collection? Can they retrieve all applicable cards in the cycle and place them in appropriate sequence? Are the children able to explain each card and retell what is happening in the life cycle?

**Next Steps:** Encourage the children to write sentences to further explain the life cycles in depth or draw their own life cycles on cards. Laminate the cards to use in free-choice time, or have them transfer their life cycle ideas into the storytelling boxes outlined in earlier activities. ■

## Grid Retells

**Materials:** large coding grid, arrow coding cards, paper, writing materials, props and loose parts to depict characters and settings from the story, paper, markers

**Instructions:** After reading a favorite book with the children, encourage them to help you complete a story web on chart paper where they can include details from the text (such as names of characters, settings, and plot). Ensure the children have a solid comprehension of the story. Ask them to sit in a large circle around the edge of a carpet or large table. Display the coding grid in the middle and invite them to help you create the setting(s) in the book on the grid using loose parts and other materials (green paper to depict grass, blue paper for water areas, a house made from blocks, and so on). Once the children are satisfied that the setting is adequately portrayed, create the characters from the story by finding a similar toy or making one from loose parts (such as a drawn or printed paper photo of the character taped on a small block). Ask the children to identify where the beginning, middle, and end of the story will occur on the coding board. Remind them of any antagonists in the text (like the fox hiding in the woods) and place these on the grid accordingly. Place the character in the beginning (or starting) location on the grid, and ask the children to provide a coding sequence to move them around the setting. As the character moves, remind the children of the story events and code the actions in the correct order to accurately retell the text. Help the character travel to the ending of the story, or the finish place on the coding board, to finish the retell.

In this story retell, the characters are drawn on grid paper and the order of their appearance as characters in the text is represented by arrow coding cards.

**Observations:** Are the children able to retell the text in logical sequence and include all relevant details? Do they articulate the retell using a beginning, middle, and end? Can the children create an accurate setting on the coding board for the story? Do they recall the story well enough to move the character on the grid? Are they able to include all plot details from the story? Do they appear engaged and comfortable? Are they interested in changing the story retell in some way to help the character or evolving it into a different version?

**Next Steps:** Encourage the children to create alternative versions of the story for retell (like fractured fairy tales). They can change or manipulate the coding board and props to reflect their new retells. The children can write their coding directions on paper for others to follow. Leave all the materials along with the text in a center for the children to continue to explore during free-choice time. ■

## Retelling Favorite Stories Using Coding Stones

**Materials:** variety of flat, smooth river rocks, acrylic paint, paintbrushes, sealant such as Mod Podge, chart paper, markers, sensory table, various loose parts from around the classroom

**Instructions:** Paint arrows on a number of flat river rocks and seal once the paint is dry. Set these aside. Encourage the children to reflect on a well-known and loved story they've explored in class. Create a story web with the children by listing various elements from the text around the web (such as characters, settings, plot, and the ending). Choose a sensory table in your classroom and help the children design and plan for how to turn the table into the setting of your story. For example, one year my students were fascinated with *Where the Wild Things Are* (Maurice Sendak). We divided the table into halves, split down the middle by a paper river. On one side was the little boy's bedroom, and on the other side was the land of the wild things. The children created the entire scene using materials from around the classroom, and what they couldn't find in toy bins they created in the art area. They created the characters by drawing pictures of each one and taping the paper on small wooden blocks to be manipulated through the scene.

Once the children have successfully created the setting and characters from the story, encourage them to lead the characters through a retell of the text from start to finish. For example, the little boy in *Where the Wild Things Are* begins the story in his bedroom. He then travels across the sea to a new land, only to return home at the end of the book. The children can plan out the story sequence by placing the arrow story stones around the sensory bin, guiding the character's actions. They can also innovate the text and rewrite the ending of the story by recording the sequence of the story stones around the setting.

**Observations:** Is the story one that the children enjoy, and does it have long-term play value? Are the children able to provide specifics from the text to create an enriched story web? Can the children adequately retell the text and make rich connections in their discussions? Are they able to design and build the setting for the story in the classroom? Do they understand the story sequence well enough to orally retell the story with enough detail to guide someone else through it? Can they place the story stones in the correct order around the setting of the story? Are the children interested in innovating the text in new directions, perhaps changing events throughout or creating a new ending?

**Next Steps:** Consider encouraging the children to code their way through the setting of a new story, or bring the play props outside for a different experience. The children can also write their own stories and retell them in the sensory bins around the classroom. They may also want to improvise stories with the stones and incorporate them into their spontaneous play in different classroom areas (such as adding them with toy dinosaurs in the sand table to direct the actions of the dinos). If creating a story setting in a sensory table is too complex, consider using a coding board and adding props to represent the setting directly on the board. ■

## Story Maps

**Materials:** paper, markers, mini paper arrows

**Instructions:** Encourage the children to draw a story map. This can be a response to a book they have read and enjoyed or a story of their own creation. Ask them to tell you their story and narrate the actions by using their finger to point to different parts of their picture in the sequence they occur. After the first retell, explain to the children that you are going to help them show the sequence of events by coding it with arrows. As the children retell the story, place paper arrows along the path to outline the actions the characters are experiencing. The first arrow should be placed at the beginning of the story, and the final arrow should be at the end. At the end of the experience, the children can glue the arrows onto the paper if so desired.

**Observations:** Is the picture drawn with detail? Can the child tell the story of what is happening on their drawing with a clear beginning, middle, and end? Can they articulate the sequence of events in order? Do they seem to understand that the arrows help tell the story of what is happening to the characters?

**Next Steps:** Encourage the children to draw larger, more complex story maps after reading detailed books together, perhaps using large construction or

A child places arrows directly on top of his drawing to show the sequence of events.

butcher paper. These stories should have a large setting and long plot. Once the picture is complete, encourage the children to retell the story together from beginning to end, and track all the movements of the character(s) by placing paper arrows on the story map. Depending on the level of complexity and detail included, this might require many arrows. Once the children are satisfied with the sequence they have created, glue the arrows in place and display the story map along with the text. Story maps can also be used as comprehension or reflection pieces after reading subsequent books together. ■

## Connecting Coding to Drawing

In coding classrooms, children are immersed in a literacy-rich environment as they explore various forms of communication and see reading and writing as tools to support their work (Umaschi Bers 2018). Educators model various forms of print, including symbolic representation, and children are encouraged to take risks and experiment with writing in different ways. Through this experience, they recognize that written symbols can communicate their ideas beyond the confines of the classroom. In the following activities, children can explore and refine this writing using a variety of unplugged activities.

## Individual Blueprint Journal

**Materials:** individual notebooks (preferably with a hard cover), writing materials including markers and crayons

**Instructions:** Keep journals in a basket in an easy-to-access location that is relevant and central to children's daily work, perhaps near the construction or art areas. The children can use these personal blueprint journals to record their ideas for building and coding work, including designs and plans for future activities, and keep records of blueprints for completed projects. Similar to how authors keep inspiration journals to jot down images and ideas for future projects, the children can use their blueprint journals as part of their design process, collecting and curating ideas over the course of the year in one place.

A child draws a picture of a train she is designing in her blueprint journal.

**Observations:** Are the children interested in recording their ideas? Do they feel ownership and pride over their work? Can they articulate the ideas they have included in their journals? Do the children share their ideas freely and easily with others? Are they able to follow through on their plans, putting them into action in construction and coding work? Do the children incorporate others' suggestions for improvement in their designs or build on previous ideas to strengthen and refine them?

**Next Steps:** Share the blueprint journals in a consolidation or reflection circle where the children voluntarily show one another their work and answer questions while asking for constructive feedback. Pay careful attention to what is shared and then help children act on their plans by gathering the necessary tools and materials in future activities so they can see their ideas turned into action. Send the journals home for family perusal, and pass them on to future teachers for continued work. ■

## Code a Letter

**Materials:** large precut upper- and lowercase alphabet letters, markers, dry-erase boards, dry-erase markers

**Instructions:** Gather the children at the carpet. Give each child a dry-erase board and marker. Tell them that you are going to code an alphabet letter and want them to draw on their dry-erase boards the sequence of instructions they hear. To help you visualize the parts that need to be described and give accurate instructions for the children to follow, hold a paper letter where the children can't see it. The purpose of the game is to see whether the children can draw what they hear and accurately identify the letter ("Draw two parallel lines on your board. Connect them in the middle by drawing a shorter line in between"). This is a complicated activity that requires the educator to be clear in their directions so the children can experience success in their drawing. Once the letter has been coded and the children have a guess on their boards, display the paper letter and once again give the coding directions, this time drawing a line on the letter with each subsequent direction. This way the children can watch you write the letter following your own code and can visualize the sequence by tracking the marker line with their eyes. Children can later trace the letters with their fingers.

A child creates the letter *p* using plastic cubes. She then draws her creation by coloring grids on paper and creating an arrow path to show the direction one follows when printing the letter.

**Observations:** Are the children able to follow your directions and make marks on their boards? Do they take risks in their learning and attempt to write a letter even when they are unsure of what it is? Do they appear comfortable and confident in the activity? Are the children able to accurately follow the sequence of steps to write a letter? Can they correctly name the letter they wrote?

**Next Steps:** Place this activity at a center for future exploration by children. If the children appear comfortable coding letters, explain an advanced version of the game where they code a number of letters sequentially to spell a short word. ■

## Alphabet (or Number) Sequence

**Materials:** large chart paper, markers

**Instructions:** Prepare the activity ahead of time. Draw a large grid (for example, 10 by 10 on one-inch grid paper). Determine a starting position on the grid and indicate this by drawing a symbol or writing a word in that square (such as a green dot or the word go). Write all the alphabet letters in random places on the grid with spaces in between. Once the grid is ready, invite the children to gather around the paper and help you code the alphabet sequence. Begin at the start location and travel horizontally and vertically along the grid until you arrive at the letter A. Record the coding directions that it took to get there. Next look for the letter B and record the coding directions it took to travel from A to B. Then proceed to C and onward until the entire alphabet is sequenced.

*Letters are written inside random squares on the grid. The alphabetic order is coded for the user to follow.*

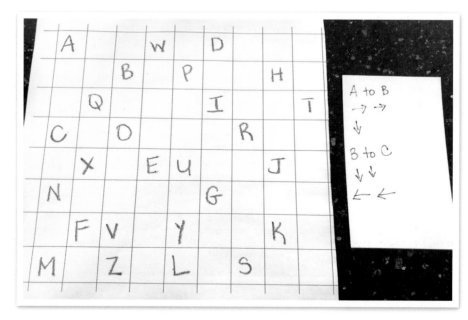

**Observations:** Are the children able to find each letter in sequence and write the coding directions? Can they reverse the process and follow prewritten instructions to locate each letter? Do they suggest other sequences to explore on the coding grid?

**Next Steps:** Adapt this activity for any sequence (such as numbers one to ten or spelling children's names in order). Provide the children with grid paper and writing tools and encourage them to create their own number and letter sequences to follow. ■

## Crack the Code

**Materials:** large chart paper, markers

**Instructions:** Prepare the activity ahead of time. Draw a large grid (for example, 10 by 10 on one-inch grid paper). Create a secret message and represent the number of letters in the answer by drawing blank spaces underneath the grid or after the question you have posed. Determine a starting position on the grid and indicate this by drawing a symbol or writing a word in that square (such as a green dot or the word *go*). Before filling in the grid with random letters, ensure the letters in your secret code are included in the grid and write them randomly and with spaces in between. This is very similar to a word search. Fill in the rest

Children follow the coding directions to reveal a classmate's name.

of your grid with random letters. Begin at the start location and code the directions for moving from letter to letter, slowly revealing the secret code. Once the grid is ready, invite the children to gather around the paper and follow the coding directions in order. As each letter is retrieved, the children can color in that section of the grid to highlight the letter, and they can also record it on the blank spaces representing the secret message. As each letter is revealed, the children can read, write, and discover the secret message.

**Observations:** Are the children able to follow the coding directions? Can they identify and copy the letter revealed in the space? Are they able to put the letters together and crack the secret code? Are they interested in writing their own messages?

**Next Steps:** Provide grid paper for the children to use in the writing center. Encourage them to create their own secret messages for friends to crack. Continue to include secret messages in your work with the children, increasing the complexity by enlarging the grid and having bigger words for them to find. ■

## Boolean Logic Guess Who!

**Materials:** whiteboards, dry-erase markers

**Instructions: Boolean logic** refers to the manipulation of binary values in computer programming, where a 1 represents the concept of "true" and a 0 represents the concept of "false." It is fundamental to operating software, but it can be an abstract concept for children to understand. In this activity, you can help the children identify the basics of Boolean logic by using the numbers 1 and 0 to represent responses to certain statements and have the children guess the mystery person. Gather the children in a whole group at the carpet. First give every child a whiteboard and dry-erase marker. Explain that you are going to state something, and if it applies to them, they write a 1 on their whiteboard. If it does not apply to them, they write a 0. Spend time guiding the children through a number of statements to help them become comfortable with the use of the number 1 as a "true" response to the statement and the number 0 to represent "false." Remind them that they are the subjects and to answer accordingly. Statements might include "I wear glasses," "I am a girl," "I have pierced ears," or "I love basketball." Once the children appear comfortable answering using Boolean logic, ask them to hand in their whiteboards. In the next game, they will be asking you the questions. Tell them that you are thinking of a mystery person in the classroom. You can write the name of that person down on a piece of paper to be revealed after the game. The children take turns asking you questions about your mystery person, including details about their appearance, personality, and behavior ( "Is the mystery person a girl?" "Does the mystery person like dogs?"). Using a whiteboard, respond to the children's statements by writing a 1 or 0 to indicate your answer to the questions. Once the children have a guess, they can suggest it. If they are correct, reveal the name of the person you had in mind as proof. If not, they can continue to ask questions until they have a guess.

Children attempt to guess who the mystery person is by examining clues and a drawing of a person.

**Observations:** Do the children understand the concept of true and false, and if not, can you modify the activity by using the terms *yes* and *no* instead? Are the children able to respond to simple questions and write their number responses independently? Can they generate their own statements when guessing who the mystery person is and share these orally or in a written format? Can they make educated guesses about who the mystery person is?

**Next Steps:** Organize this activity into a center for children to explore during free-choice time, or use it as a small-group activity. In place of a mystery person, place a mystery object inside a box or bag and have the children guess what it is.

Many classes also use a show-and-tell time where children can present objects from their homes to their peers. Incorporating Boolean language into these activities is a good way to differentiate them and infuse some computational thinking. ■

## ASCII Code with Plastic Bricks

**Materials:** large collection of plastic bricks, such as Legos, a large click-in mat for the bricks, mini alphabet cards, paper, writing tools

**Instructions:** Before introducing the activity to the children, create an alphabet legend on the mat. Designate each letter of the alphabet with a different brick. You can also create a simple message for children to decode (for example, in the photo the secret message reads "little cat"). This activity would be best implemented with a pair of children or as an independent task. Explain to the children that computers use a special language to communicate called ASCII and that they are going to learn to communicate in codes like computer programmers do. Show them the brick legend and explain that each letter in their secret message is going to be represented with a special brick. The bricks need to be carefully selected, because if the wrong one is used in the secret code, the reader will not be able to accurately understand it. Demonstrate how certain bricks can be put together to form certain words or sentences. Invite the children to think about how they might write their name or a simple message for others to read, and explain which bricks they would use to represent these.

Each letter of the alphabet is represented by a different plastic brick. Children build codes for one another to solve.

Once the children appear to understand the concept, place the materials in a center for further exploration. The children can use the paper and writing materials to transpose the brick messages into traditional writing or plan out their secret code before creating it with bricks.

**Observations:** Are the children interested in the activity? Do they understand the concept of a legend and how their ideas can be translated by using different bricks? Are they able to represent a simple word or sentence using one brick per letter, separating words with spaces?

**Next Steps:** Offer suggestions for differentiating the activity based on student need (such as creating first names or writing complex phrases). The children can take photos of their codes, which can be placed in a center for decoding by their peers. Consider reaching out to others by using social media to share your brick codes, asking them to solve your messages, and inviting them to send your class messages to decode. Replace the alphabet with numbers, and ask the children to explore math concepts using the secret codes.                ■

## Engaging Children in Literacy

Incorporating coding into regular drawing, reading, and writing activities can make literacy enjoyable for all children. Interactive games and activities that encourage children to explore, retell, and innovate texts can help improve comprehension. Children can use coding materials to tell their own stories while exploring concepts of print more fully. Coding is a universal language used to help children connect with others from all around the world!

**CHAPTER 8**

# Coding to Encourage Playful Math

*A flurry of activity was taking place on the carpet as the children worked to build
a complex city using blocks and pentominoes. After running out of car tracks,
they searched the room for a replacement.*

*"These should work! They look just like little roads."*

*"I can connect them end to end. Then we can have side streets too."*

*"The mini cars fit right on them. If we want to give directions to drivers,
we can code their path."*

*After the children built a complex system of roads, they decided it would be
easy to give directions to one another to help navigate the path.*

*"Go down three and right four and you'll get to the grocery store!"*

*Seeing how they incorporated their understanding of pentominoes and coding
to enhance their building experience was interesting.*

Consider your math program. If a visitor were to walk into your classroom, what messages would the organization of the environment, student relationships, recent explorations, and documentation on display share about how you and your students feel about math? How do you ensure that standards and accountability are being met while still engaging children in authentic experiences that build their confidence and fluency and help connect concepts to the real world? Children who are immersed in a mathematically authentic and complex learning environment will become confident producers of information, integrating their understandings of number concepts and relationships into collaborative and relevant learning experiences (Moss 2016). Coding can help children see math as more than a function to be performed or a problem to be solved; it can help them see themselves as mathematical constructors, putting the emphasis on the process of exploration rather than on just a final correct response. If we believe in the Reggio Emilia foundation that children are capable learners who are curious and enjoy connecting with others in meaningful learning opportunities, then we will also value the role that authentic math has in the classroom. In my experience, young children who experiment with coding benefit mathematically from challenging situations. Not only are they able to engage in the problem-solving process as they design, test, refine, and communicate their programs to others, but they also can use mathematical tools and concepts to explore the games and activities. Coding becomes one of the Reggio Emilia hundreds of languages used to explore, understand, and articulate the math learning happening within activities.

In working with children over the years, I've realized that coding can supplement one's math program and encourage confident and joyful math experiences in a variety of ways:

> **Coding helps children visualize abstract math.** Young children are often not interested or developmentally ready or able to read questions or manipulate writing tools to complete worksheets. Paperwork often takes math out of context and isolates it in tasks to be completed by children. It may not be relevant or meaningful to children. When we implement math into coding work, children are able to use their previous knowledge and understanding about numeracy and spatial relationships and incorporate these into their games and activities to maneuver around a grid or share their algorithms with others. Their learning becomes spiraled as they integrate math concepts into subsequent coding activities, refining and enhancing their understanding over time. Control structures integrate multiple concepts into coding experiences (for example, looping infuses patterning into the coding work), giving children tangible ways to explore and manipulate abstract math concepts. The math becomes alive, serving a purpose to help solve a problem or communicate a message to a greater audience.

> **Coding helps kids see the relationship that math has to the real world.** By understanding coding's place and relevance in everyday objects, children can see and appreciate the importance of math firsthand. They recognize that math is an integral part of their programming and is necessary to successfully communicate their thinking in computational ways. Community partners can assist with this process by speaking to children about how math and computational thinking are used each day in their own personal and professional lives and offer guidance to children in classroom activities whenever applicable.

> **Coding helps kids see the beauty and intricacy in math.** Math is found everywhere in the natural world, and just as an artist appreciates the process of creating and communicating through an aesthetic language, mathematicians seek to discover and understand intricate patterns in our natural world. Mathematicians often describe their work as "beautiful" and "elegant" and are continually seeking new and enlightened ways of exploring problems in the world around them. Children who use coding in their math work can also experience this same level of satisfaction and enjoyment when exploring integrated computational activities, especially those

that produce aesthetic results that can be valued for the process of their creation as well as their beautiful end results. This is evident in the many artistic coding activities children can experience, and it can be enhanced further when children learn to code using computers in subsequent activities.

> **Coding encourages multiple entry points for kids (low floor, high ceiling).** When engaging children in math activities in the classroom, it is important to provide open-ended tasks that invite all to engage as active participants. Boaler (2016) refers to these as "low floor, high ceiling" activities because they are open enough to invite all children to connect in some initial way and deep enough that the learning can grow in multiple directions. Children can work at different paces and depths of engagement at the same time. The activities are differentiated so that multiple ways of knowing and being are included and children can evolve the tasks based on their own interests, strengths, and needs. Unlike traditional math tasks that have one correct response, coding activities that incorporate low floor–high ceiling tasks have specific criteria: the process of learning is more important than the answer to the problem itself; all students can access the problem in some capacity; children have room to move toward exploring more complex math concepts at higher levels of engagement in the same problem; and the process provides an opportunity for children to engage in rich math discourse.

> **Coding encourages children to become confident and invested mathematicians.** Coding can also foster collaborative problem-solving in math activities where children work together to solve a complex problem. Unlike traditional math that focuses on individual student work and the arrival at one correct answer, coding is a social activity in which children strategize and problem solve in small groups and consider multiple paths of action to arrive at a shared goal. Reggio Emilia–inspired environments promote and encourage cooperative math activities in which children support one another in complex coding tasks, incorporating their individual strengths and interests for the greater good of the group. They become confident as they share their expertise and grow their repertoire of computational interests and abilities. Children work toward the shared goals of all coders and become deeply invested in their explorations together. Growth mindset is encouraged as children realize they can achieve more successful coding work with a positive attitude, dedicated and sustained work, and help from more experienced peers and adults.

> **Coding encourages problem-solving.** In addition to the authentic math opportunities that present themselves in coding explorations and activities, educators can also engage children in explicit instruction that helps build

their schema, fulfills curriculum standards, and inspires them to integrate more complex problem-solving into their subsequent work. The design process encourages rich problem-solving regardless of whether children are solving a teacher-initiated challenge outlined in a game or activity or are using coding as a language for exploring and communicating their ideas to others in a self-directed project or inquiry. After encountering a problem, children create a plan for how to proceed and gather necessary resources and materials. Using background knowledge and support from peers or an educator, children can tinker with the materials and create their coding project. As they experiment, they are able to self-assess and see whether the project is working as envisioned. If not, they can test the design and uncover bugs to improve the program. Once a final project is created, children are then able to share their work with others, communicating their new understandings beyond the walls of the classroom and perhaps inspiring others to try to code in a similar way.

> **Coding makes math work fun and engaging.** In addition to embedding numerous math concepts and a growth mindset into engaging activities, coding can be a very motivating way to help children sustain interest in complex math problems. Cultivating a safe and supportive environment that promotes risk-taking and mistake making as learning opportunities, children are invited to sustain interest in enjoyable yet challenging activities. Umaschi Bers (2018) describes this as "hard fun . . . an activity that engages [children] because it is both enjoyable and challenging" (92). Children are motivated by their social and emotional investment in the activity and desire to succeed, and these help them persevere even when the coding experience might be difficult or problematic. Unlike rote math tasks that might intimidate children or cause anxiety (such as worksheets or drills), difficult coding experiences that are supported by an engaged educator can build resilience and determination in children's math explorations.

## Connecting Coding to Number Sense

Just as coding can help improve literacy skills through alphabet activities, children's number sense can be improved through unplugged coding (Moss 2016). Building subitizing skills and encouraging children to explore and internalize number relationships helps them become accurate, confident, and fluent mathematicians. Subitizing is the ability to instantly recognize the quantity of objects in a set without counting them. There are many coding activities that help achieve these goals and can be differentiated to meet the needs of all learners.

## Coding on Ten Frames

**Materials:** large ten frame, blocks, arrow coding cards

**Instructions:** Create a large ten frame on the ground using tape or chalk. Determine a starting position, usually the square representing the 1 on the ten frame. Add one or two blocks as obstacles. Ask a child to volunteer to be the player and have them stand on the starting position. Demonstrate how the player can be coded around the grid from the number 1 position all the way to the end position or number 10. As you program the player, represent the code by placing the arrow coding cards next to the ten frame. Add additional blocks as barriers in subsequent games.

*Large foam puzzle mats can easily be turned into a ten frame for outdoor play.*

**Observations:** Do the children recognize the number placements on a ten frame? Can they locate them? Do they understand the purpose of the game is to move from the 1 position to the 10 position? Can they follow the directions? Are they able to become the programmer and code their friends around the grid?

**Next Steps:** Add another ten frame and ask the children to identify all number spots (1 through 20). Add obstacles and challenge the children to program one another through the frames and move from the starting to the ending position. Once the children are comfortable, change the starting and ending location to different numbers (18 to 3, for example). They can move forward or backward through the grid. Continue to add ten frames for an extra challenge as the children have more places to move and higher numbers to consider. ■

## Coding on the Hundreds Grid

**Materials:** multiple copies of individual hundreds grids, writing materials, dice

**Instructions:** Explain to the children that they will be coding number paths inside the grid. If you are using one die, write the numbers 1 to 6 anywhere inside the grid. If you are using two dice, write the numbers 1 to 12 anywhere inside the grid. Roll the dice for a starting point and again for a stopping point. Demonstrate to the children that they can code their way around the grid, connecting the two rolled numbers using the shortest/fastest path possible by drawing arrows to indicate direction inside each individual square on the grid. Draw each path using a different color of marker or crayon to help it stand out from the others. Challenge the children to roll and create as many different paths as they can.

*After writing the numbers on the grid, two dice are rolled and a path to travel from one to the other is coded.*

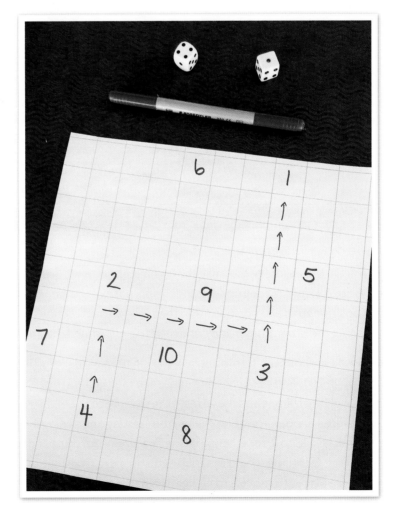

**Observations:** Are the children able to recognize the numbers rolled? Can they identify where they are located on the grid? Do they see a clear path between the two numbers? Are they able to draw arrows independently and in a path to indicate movement from one number to the next? What do the children do when they encounter a square needed for a path that is already used for a previous one? Can they strategize how to move around the path or incorporate the previous path into the new one?

**Next Steps:** Differentiate this experience by increasing the number of dice rolled and including more numbers within the grid. This challenges children to work with adding larger numbers. Create a grid outside using tape or chalk. The children can indicate the path taken by placing arrow coding cards inside the grid. ■

## Superhero Rescue

**Materials:** grid paper, character stickers, writing materials

**Instructions:** Encourage the children to choose two stickers—one to represent the hero and another to represent someone who needs to be rescued. The children place the two stickers apart from each other on the grid. Draw obstacles inside many of the squares. Determine the hero character and the character to be rescued and encourage the children to draw a coding path avoiding the obstacles. Count how many squares are needed in the path. Choose a different color marker or crayon and create a different path from start to finish. Count and record the number of squares needed for the new path, and repeat the process over and over. See which paths were the shortest and the longest. Decide which path would be the best rescue path for the hero character to take.

**Observations:** Are the children able to maneuver around the obstacles? Can they plan out, count, and record the different paths their characters can take? Are they able to determine the most and least efficient paths?

**Next Steps:** Differentiate the activity by providing larger or smaller grids, depending on the needs of your children. Remove the obstacles if the children find they are cumbersome at first. To provide an extra challenge, add a variety of stops along the way for characters (for example, before arriving at the final character, they must first stop to get food). Create the rescue grid on the ground using tape or chalk, and place real objects as characters (like a fire truck, dolls, stuffed animals, or cars). The children can use arrow coding cards to track the different paths taken. ■

*Three different paths are coded on the grid paper. The number of arrows used is calculated to determine the shortest path.*

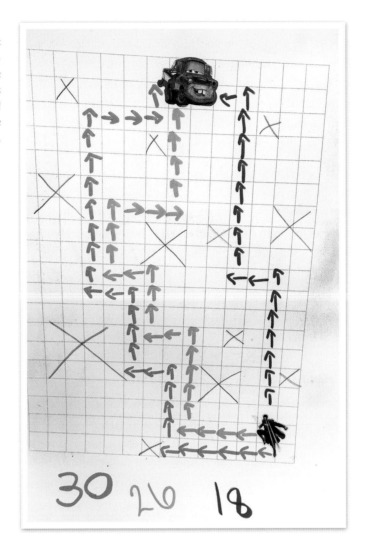

## Find the Treasure

**Materials:** large piece of paper, sticky notes, stickers, pointer, pocket chart, arrow coding cards

**Instructions:** Prepare the activity ahead of time by creating a complex array of sticky notes. Hide one sticker beneath a sticky note (place it on the back of the note). Determine a starting place. Introduce the activity to the children by explaining that they will be looking for the treasure hidden behind a paper. Demonstrate to them how they can code one another around the grid by giving directions. Ask a child to volunteer and help them place the pointer on the starting location. Give the child multiple sequential directions to follow (move right two spaces, move down four spaces). The child tracks the spaces traveled by pointing to each with the pointer. When the coder has finished giving the directions, the child being programmed lifts up the note to see if a sticker is revealed underneath. If it is, the treasure has been found. If not, give further coding directions to move around the grid. Directions can be recorded by the programmer by placing the arrow coding cards in the pocket chart as they are used. Once the treasure is found, have the children turn their heads or close their eyes and move the sticky note with the treasure to a new location on the grid.

A sticker is hidden underneath one of the cards. Children code one another to a card, then flip it over to see if the sticker is below.

**Observations:** Are the children able to give and receive directions? Can they accurately follow and point to each space as it's counted by the programmer? Do they understand the concept of the game? Do they persevere if it takes a long time to discover the treasure? Can they place the arrow coding cards in the pocket using different lines to represent each direction?

**Next Steps:** Differentiate the number of spaces in the grid based on student needs (fewer or more sticky notes included). Place multiple treasures in the grid if the children have a difficult time waiting to locate them. You can also create the grid on the ground using index cards in place of sticky notes. This way children can easily change the format of the array and hide the treasure from their peers. ■

## Collect the Hearts

**Materials:** large coding grid, arrow coding cards, hearts (or other treasures to collect, such as gold coins or gems), characters (photos of children taped to blocks or minifigures)

**Instructions:** Place the hearts around the grid. Determine a starting location. Have the children play in pairs against one another. In each pair, there is one programmer and one player. The programmer must direct their player around the grid to retrieve as many hearts as possible. One direction can be given at a time, and then the turn is passed to the other team. Programmers cannot direct their player into an occupied square on the grid. The team that collects the most hearts at the end wins the game.

A character is drawn on a piece of paper and taped to a block. The character is maneuvered around the grid, collecting as many hearts as possible.

**Observations:** Do the children understand the concept of the game? Can programmers direct their players clearly and accurately around the grid? Do the children understand and implement the rules (not using an occupied square, one code given at a time) fairly? Can they count and compare their hearts at the end of the game to determine the winner?

**Next Steps:** Challenge the children by placing obstacles within the grid that need to be avoided when collecting the treasure. Increase or decrease the size of the grid depending on the needs of the children. Bring the game outdoors for further learning, with natural items (sticks, pine cones, leaves) used as treasures. ∎

## Can You Build It?

**Materials:** blocks or connecting cubes, premade building sequencing cards, blank sequencing cards, writing tools

**Instructions:** Educators can prepare ahead of time for this activity by creating building sequencing cards that challenge the children to follow directions in a number of ways. Introduce the activity to the children by explaining that they are going to use a number code to help them construct with the blocks. Present one coding card and demonstrate how each number in the sequence indicates the number of blocks to be used in that tower. The children can start slowly with simple rows of blocks and progress to more complex arrangements by increasing the array of numbers being used. Once they are comfortable following the building code, encourage them to use blank cards and write their own codes for a peer to follow.

Each tower is represented by the number of cubes used to build it.

**Observations:** Are the children able to conceptualize the written number code as a building plan and use it to create a block structure? Can they create their own complex codes for others to follow? What other ideas do the children have for representing their building ideas as programs for others to follow?

**Next Steps:** Challenge the children to follow and create more complex codes. Perhaps they can create and build various lines of code (two or more rows combined together). Ask the children what other building materials they'd like to use. Challenge them to use the code to create recognizable structures (for example, in place of simple towers, perhaps they build a growing pattern or create a house). Take photos of the children's creations and post them with the code for others to follow. Perhaps create a coding book that children can access during free-choice time and continue to add to over the course of the year. ■

## Sorting Algorithms Game

**Materials:** sorting algorithm mat, mini number cards, one die

**Instructions:** Explain to the children that a **sorting algorithm** is a way for a computer to reorganize a large number of items into a specific order (alphabetical, highest-to-lowest, shortest-to-longest, biggest-to-smallest, and so on). Sorting algorithms take a large list of items as **input data**, perform a specific operation or operations on them, and produce ordered arrays as output data. Children can practice physically manipulating data, represented as objects, and use an algorithm mat to dramatize the operations a computer might take to sort the data. In this activity, place mini number cards randomly on the left-hand side of the mat. Each number can be moved forward one space at a time and only into empty places on the mat. Roll the die and identify the number. Locate that mini number card and move it forward one place. The purpose is to move all mini number cards from the left-hand side of the mat into an ordered list on the right.

**Observations:** Do the children recognize the numbers rolled on the die? Can they identify the corresponding mini number card? Do they understand that the cards can only move into one spot at a time and cannot be moved if they are blocked by another number? Can the children successfully move the cards across the mat so they are listed in correct order on the right-hand side?

**Next Steps:** Use different representations of data to be sorted on the template using loose parts (such as different colors or sizes of pompoms). Ask the children what games they envision playing using the template—they may have some interesting ideas to share. Sorting algorithm templates can also be a fun and easy game to play outdoors or in the gym. Create the template with tape

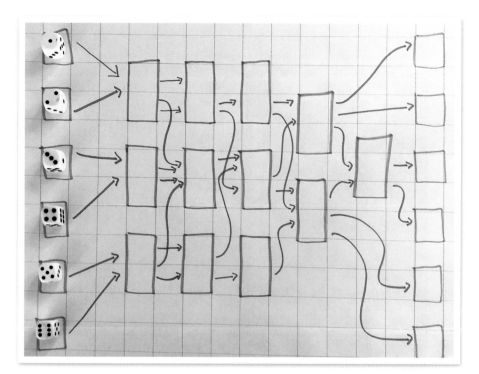

*Children take turns moving the dice one at a time until they cross through the maze and arrive at the other side.*

or chalk and encourage the children to dramatize data by placing themselves in the spaces on the left side (or input area) of the template. They can move themselves through the grid, with or without rolling a die to see how many places to move, and sort themselves in different ways on the other side. ■

## Roll and Race

**Materials:** yarn, square tiles, dice

**Instructions:** One or two children can play this game. Create a line using yarn. Each player chooses a side and takes a turn rolling their dice. The player subitizes the pips on the dice and then places that number of squares on their side of the yarn. Players keep rolling and adding squares until they reach the end of the length of yarn. The player with the most tiles in a row wins.

**Observations:** Can the children subitize their number and add the corresponding number of squares to their side of the yarn? Is the game too easy or too challenging for them? What other ideas do the children have for enhancing the game?

*Two children play
Roll and Race.*

**Next Steps:** Provide a longer length of yarn to increase the difficulty of the game. You can also use multiple dice, which requires the children to add more numbers together. ■

## Pentomino Puzzles

**Materials:** large collection of pentominoes, pentomino puzzle mats (total number of squares must be divisible by five)

**Instructions:** Create the pentomino puzzle mats ahead of time using large grid paper. Laminate each puzzle for durability. Working with pentominoes helps children practice persevering in challenging tasks and debugging problems with the arrangement of their pieces, promoting computational thinking. Encourage the children to spend time working with each piece, attempting to fit them together without leaving any gaps in the puzzle.

**Observations:** Are the children able to rotate and fit together the pentomino pieces? Do they persevere with the same puzzle over time? How do they respond when feeling challenged? Do they work together in pairs to collaborate on the same puzzle?

**Next Steps:** Offer the children a variety of sizes of puzzle mats and encourage them to work together to solve each. A very large mat can be offered as a collaborative center, and the children can work on the puzzle at their leisure, leaving fitted pieces in place so the next visitor can continue working on the puzzle without starting over. ■

## Coding Dice

**Materials:** variety of wooden blocks, game pieces, large coding grid

**Instructions:** Transform the wooden blocks into coding dice by writing directions and numbers on each. Present the dice, game pieces, and large coding board to the children and ask for their suggestions regarding how the materials can be used and what types of games they might like to play. Place the materials at a table during free-choice time and invite the children to visit, creating their own games and activities. During the next whole-group circle, ask the children to share the different games they created using the loose parts.

*Coding dice can easily be made by writing on wooden cubes with permanent marker.*

**Observations:** Are the children interested in manipulating the coding pieces? What types of games and activities do they play? What are the guidelines or rules for the games? Are the children willing to share their ideas during whole-group conversations?

**Next Steps:** Take the children's ideas and help transform them into real games. Gather materials if needed and play the new games together with the children. Gather documentation of the games to share during circle time so that all children can observe the game in action and understand how to play it. Offer the new games and activities at centers during the next free-choice activity time. ■

## Build a Grid Shape

**Materials:** coding grid, letter cards, number cards, colorful squares of paper that fit inside the grid sections, dry-erase board, dry-erase marker

**Instructions:** Display the coding grid in the center of a large working space so that all children have a clear view. Place the letter cards along the *x* axis (horizontal line) and the number cards along the *y* axis (vertical line). Explain to the children that each line has a specific name. When the *x*-axis and *y*-axis lines intersect, they form a coordinate. Demonstrate this by choosing a specific coordinate pair, articulating it aloud, and using your hands to run along the lines to where they intersect. Place a colorful square in that space on the grid and write the matching coordinate on the dry-erase board. Explain to the children that they can create shapes and pictures by filling in certain sections of the grid. Continue to add more squares and write the corresponding coordinates until you create a larger shape on the grid (like a rectangle). Remove the squares. Encourage the children to add their own squares to the grid and write the corresponding coordinates, creating their own unique shapes and designs.

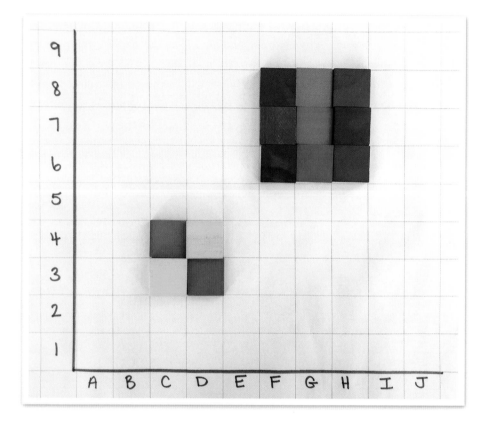

Different shapes and designs can be created on the grid. Coordinates can be found for each tile.

**Observations:** Do the children understand the relationship between the coordinates written on the dry-erase board and their matching place on the grid? Can the children place square papers on the grid to form a unique shape or design? Can they lead one another in placing the squares on the grid by writing the coordinate directions on the dry-erase board?

**Next Steps:** Leave the grid and corresponding materials out on a table during free-choice time for the children to explore. Create a positive and negative horizontal axis and encourage the children to create symmetrical designs on the grid. Ask the children what other games they think of when working with the grid. Take photos of their work and share their ideas and experiences during the next whole-group consolidation circle. ■

## Pentomino Coding Path

**Materials:** grid paper, large collection of pentominoes, coding characters (such as loose parts, minifigures, or toy animals)

**Instructions:** Display the coding grid paper for the children and place two coding characters apart from each other on the grid. Using the pentominoes, attempt to create a coding path by placing each piece so it is touching the next, zig-zagging across the grid to the next player. This will be quite challenging for the children because pentominoes will create "dead ends," and the pieces must fit together to form a path from start to finish. Unlike the other coding paths in this book, the purpose of this game is to puzzle the pentominoes together to create a path, regardless of how many pieces or squares in the grid it takes. The emphasis is on spatial awareness and logic.

*A path for the mini vehicle is created by connecting pentominoes end to end.*

**Observations:** Are the children able to conceptualize the use of the pentominoes as a kind of coding path? Do they see how the pieces can fit together end to end to form a path? Do they persevere when challenged in the activity? Are they willing to take their paths apart and try different ways of solving the code when they get stuck in the process? How many different ways can the children create paths for the characters?

**Next Steps:** Encourage the children to explore the materials further by placing them on a table during free-choice time. Increase or decrease the size of the grid or number of pentominoes offered to differentiate the activity. Place obstacles inside the grid for an additional challenge. ∎

Unplugged coding activities are a versatile way to engage children in complex, multifaceted math activities that capitalize on their interests, and they can be differentiated to meet children's needs. All areas can be easily integrated, resulting in authentic and layered math experiences that all learners can enjoy.

# References

Aspinall, Brian. 2017. *Code Breakers: Increase Creativity, Remix Assessment, and Develop a Class of Coder Ninjas!* San Diego: Dave Burgess Consulting.

Bitesize. 2018. "Introduction to Computational Thinking." BBC. www.bbc.com /education/guides/zp92mp3/revision. Accessed February 13, 2020.

Boaler, Jo. 2016. *Mathematical Mindsets: Understanding Students' Potential through Creative Math, Inspiring Messages, and Innovative Teaching.* San Francisco: Jossey-Bass.

Bruner, Jerome. 1960. *The Process of Education.* New York: Vintage Books.

Burns, Marilyn. 1994. *The Greedy Triangle.* New York: Scholastic.

Dewey, John. 1916. *Democracy and Education: An Introduction to the Philosophy of Education.* New York: Macmillan.

Dietze, B., and D. Kashin. 2018. *Playing and Learning in Early Childhood Education.* 2nd ed. North York, ON: Pearson Canada.

Flemming, Laura. 2015. *Worlds of Making: Best Practices for Establishing a Makerspace for Your School.* Thousand Oaks, CA: Corwin.

Heick, Terry. 2019. "4 Phases of Inquiry-Based Learning: A Guide for Teachers." TeachThought. Last modified November 5, 2019. www.teachthought.com /pedagogy/4-phases-inquiry-based-learning-guide-teachers.

IBM Knowledge Center. 2019. "ASCII, Decimal, Hexadecimal, Octal, and Binary Conversion Table." IBM Knowledge Center. www.ibm.com/support /knowledgecenter/en/ssw_aix_72/network/conversion_table.html. Accessed February 13, 2020.

Isenberg, Joan Packer, and Mary Renck Jalongo. 2018. *Creative and Arts-Based Learning: Preschool through Fourth Grade.* 7th ed. New York: Pearson.

Kang, Jinju. 2007. "How Many Languages Can Reggio Children Speak? Many More Than a Hundred!" *Gifted Child Today* 30 (3): 45–48, 65.

Moss, Joan, Catherine D. Bruce, Bev Caswell, Tara Flynn, and Zachary Hawes. 2016. *Taking Shape: Activities to Develop Geometric and Spatial Thinking, Grades K–2.* Toronto: Pearson.

National Research Council. 2012. *Education for Life and Work: Developing Transferable Knowledge and Skills in the 21st Century.* Washington, DC: National Academies

Press. http://sites.nationalacademies.org/cs/groups/dbassesite/documents /webpage/dbasse_070895.pdf.

Pecaski McLennan, Deanna Marie. 2008. "The Benefits of Using Sociodrama in the Elementary Classroom: Promoting Caring Relationships among Educators and Students." *Early Childhood Education Journal* 35 (5): 451–56.

———. 2009. "Ten Ways to Create a More Democratic Classroom." *Young Children* 64 (4): 100–101.

———. 2012. "Using Sociodrama to Help Young Children Problem Solve." *Early Childhood Education Journal* 39 (6): 407–12.

———. 2017a. "Creating Coding Stories and Games." *Teaching Young Children* 10 (3): 18–21.

———. 2017b. "Now Read This: Books That Introduce Coding to Children. *Teaching Young Children* 10 (3): 22–23.

Piaget, Jean. 1936. *Origins of Intelligence in the Child*. London: Routledge & Kegan Paul.

Stadler, Marie A., and Gay Cuming Ward. 2005. "Supporting the Narrative Development of Young Children." *Early Childhood Education Journal* 33 (2): 73–80.

Tarr, Patricia. 2001. "Aesthetic Codes in Early Childhood Classrooms: What Art Educators Can Learn from Reggio Emilia." *Art Education* 54 (3): 33–39.

Umaschi Bers, Marina. 2018. *Coding as a Playground: Programming and Computational Thinking in the Early Childhood Classroom*. New York: Routledge.

Vygotsky, Lev S. 1962. *Thought and Language*. Cambridge, MA: MIT Press.

Wein, Carol Anne. 2008. *Emergent Curriculum in the Primary Classroom: Interpreting the Reggio Emilia Approach in Schools*. New York: Teachers College Press.

———. 2014. *The Power of Emergent Curriculum: Stories from Early Childhood Settings*. Washington, DC: National Association for the Education of Young Children.

Weisman Topal, Cathy, and Lella Gandini. 1999. *Beautiful Stuff!: Learning with Found Materials*. Worchester, MA: Davis Publications.

Wexler, Alice. 2004. "A Theory for Living: Walking with Reggio Emilia." *Art Education* 57 (6): 13–19.

Wing, Jeannette M. 2006. "Computational Thinking." *Communications of the ACM* 49 (3): 33–35.

Wurm, Julianne P. 2005. *Working in the Reggio Way: A Beginner's Guide for American Teachers*. Saint Paul, MN: Redleaf Press.

# Index